MW00716614

The New
Marriage Paradigm

Inspiring the Transformation and
Evolution of Committed Relationships

Moreah Ragusa

Copyright © 2006 Moreah Ragusa

Published by:
The Phoenix Coaching and Transformation Corporation
11550 - 44 Street SE, Calgary, Alberta, Canada T2Z 4A2

Cover design, text layout, and graphics by Shelley Hedges
Edited by Simone Gabbay
Author photo by Carolyn Sandstrom

Reproduction in whole or in part, in any form, including
storage in memory device systems, is forbidden without
written permission, except that portions may be used in
broadcast or printed commentary or review when attributed
fully to author and publication by names.

First Printing, May 2006
Printed in Canada

ISBN   0-9781145-0-7 (Canada)
          0-9777106-9-6 (USA)

1. Psychology.   2. Relationship.   3. Self-Help.   I. Title.

Inquiries, orders, and other requests should be addressed to:
The Phoenix Coaching and Transformation Corporation
11550 - 44 Street SE, Calgary, Alberta, Canada T2Z 4A2
Phone 403-278-3700
E-mail: info@thephoenixcoaching.com

www.thephoenixcoaching.com

May you discover
that we are all destined to love,
because we can only know
what we really are
through loving the self.
And that is accomplished only
through loving another.

With Gratitude and Love,
Moreah

The *trinity knot* depicted on the cover and at chapter
beginnings is an ancient symbol representing the
eternal nature of love and relationships, as explored
in *The New Marriage Paradigm.*

Table of Contents

vii   *Acknowledgments*
ix   *Preface*
xiii   *Introduction*

1   **Chapter One: Why We Marry**
       Love and Fear
       Communicating Truthfully
       Security and Ideals

9   **Chapter Two: Why We Divorce**
       Ego Nudgings
       The Authentic Voice of Spirit
       The Importance of Feeling Valued

15   **Chapter Three: The New vs. the Old
Paradigm of Marriage**
       Soul-Filled Love
       Expansive and Inclusive Love
       Cause and Effect

25   **Chapter Four: Chemistry, Fire, and Intimacy**
       Encountering Fire
       The Chemistry of Passionate Love
       The Quest for Power and Control
       Transparency and Tears
       The Dynamics of Sexual Violation
          Energy

51   **Chapter Five: Why We Marry "Our Parents"**
         Owning the Disowned
         The Dynamics of Projection
         The CAB Principle©
         The Fantasy of the Ideal Mate

69   **Chapter Six: How Values Drive**
         Relationships
             Love Knows No Judgment
             Identifying Couple Values
             Remodeling Relationships

89   **Chapter Seven: Communication**
             The Macro-Self vs. the Ego-Self
             Sharing Secrets
             Nurturing Intimacy

105   **Chapter Eight: The Question of Fidelity**
             Emotional Hunger and Infidelity
             Two Identities—Two Sets of Rules
             Evolving through Love
             Morals, Values, Traits, and Beliefs
             Yearning for Home
             Time Passages to Freedom or Guilt
             Fidelity and Love
             Our Greater Self
             The True Purpose of the Body

141   **Chapter Nine: Inseparable Energies—**
         A Sacred Dance
             The Power of Surrender
             Balancing Head and Heart
             Maturing through the Feminine

161   **Chapter Ten: Sacred Union**
          Truthful Conversations
          Power and the Need to Be Right
          Receiving and Expressing Anger and
              Sadness
          Destructive Inner Dialogues
          Parenting Style Differences
          Trust—Financial and Emotional
          Assuming and Withholding
          Prioritizing and "Self-Fullness"

197   **Chapter Eleven: The Soulmates' Final Dance**
          Two Souls—One Light

203   **Epilogue**
          Soul to Soul

Acknowledgments

First and foremost, I would like to thank my devoted and cherished "dance partner," Doug (whom the reader will meet as "Allan" in this book), who fearlessly continues to walk beside me, allowing us to heal our wounds and destructive patterns. To you, I am eternally grateful for the view you hold of me which has proven to me that I am indeed both lovable and valuable. Thank you, too, for guiding, supporting, and parenting my children.

Thanks to Simone Gabbay, the editor of all my written works, whose tireless love, commitment, and encouragement have shaped me as a writer.

Last but not least, I wish to thank Shelley Hedges for creating the beautiful cover design, which illuminates the heart and soul of the message within this book.

There is no more lovely, friendly,
and charming relationship, communion,
or company than a good marriage.

Martin Luther

Preface

My work as a practicing psychotherapist in large part involves understanding the dynamics of the heart and mind as they pertain to relationships—more specifically, romantic ones. Over the past ten years, I have paid particular attention to the dominant issues that arise while we are in love. Currently in the eleventh year of my third marriage,[1] I have encountered many issues that were similar to those reported by my clients, and I have felt some keen desires and frustrations emerging. These sentiments simply wouldn't be suppressed or ignored any longer, so I began to explore their impact and to identify ways in which they were transforming me, and, because they are universal, the ways in which they were transforming how and why we love.

Some of the key issues that I will share in this book are aspects of intimacy, flirtation, chemistry, communication, secrets, values and priorities, the differing attractions we feel, commitment, fidelity,

---

[1] Please see my autobiography, *Our Cosmic Dance*, for background information.

monogamy, soul inter-dependence, and blending families.

I believe that some of the needs couples are facing and feeling today have been around for centuries, while others are indicative of the heightened opportunities that relationships offer the soul for its growth and awakening to its authentic power. Some yearnings are ancient, such as the desire for intimacy, which, ironically, is often accompanied by fear of intimacy. A more recent demand on love relation-ships is a heightened longing for a partner who is willing to play and integrate the different roles of lover, friend, spiritual companion, financial partner, co-parent, and teacher.

I believe that it is the search for such a perfect mate "out there" that has driven the marriage/divorce rates to a 50 percent margin. This means that half of us are not willing to remain in marriages that do not fulfill our needs—yet we want to find a relationship that will.

Now that many of us have bounced around searching for the ready-made "ideal mate" and discovered that they don't exist, we have wised up and, instead, we now work on transforming ourselves into extraordinarily dynamic and versatile beings. For many years, the idea of an ideal mate seemed unattainable, so we settled; but now we are not settling, rather, we are nurturing the fullest expressions of being in each other—drawing out the most mature masculine and feminine qualities. Both men and women have role-swapped enough to see that both sexes have their fair share of chal-lenges. Consequently, a deeper understanding of, and compassion for, our differences are creating a fertile ground from which can spring forth a new and deeper love.

The soul seeks truth, freedom, openness, expression, appreciation, creativity, and intimacy, while the ego avoids them at all cost. This split in soul-need vs. ego-avoidance creates a dichotomy of goals that leaves the individuals within this dance feeling torn and confused. Therefore, it is my sincerest hope that this book will serve as a guide, placing stepping stones through the troubled waters of your romantic endeavors.

You can't describe love,
you can only live it!

Cynthia Carragher

Introduction

The institution of marriage has molded and twisted to conform to the needs of the souls growing within its parameters. Over the millennia, marriage, women, men, and the social power and influence they bring to mankind have also shifted and fluctuated. Because neither the human soul nor the marriage paradigm itself is static, we should wisely reexamine the need for change to parallel the respective growth of each.

I set out to do some research. I examined anthropological information, as well as research detailing brain chemistry changes, and considered them in the context of ongoing concerns of couples who are in love. I explored romance, security, and marriage and concluded that the institution of marriage is undergoing a deep transformation to facilitate evolutionary gains of the partners' souls. As a result of this process, marriage is expanding to encompass the couple's new requirements.

The most profound need that must be addressed in the new marriage paradigm is that the marriage has to support both the independence and interdependence of the mates within it. This means that each soul must know with certainty that they can create a fulfilling and abundant life independently of the other, while also being confident that they can help each other to grow and uncover whatever blocks their hearts from loving the other more completely. The result will be a richer appreciation and acceptance for both their biological and global family members.

The new marriage paradigm does not separate the love it creates within its playground from the world; instead, it extends it unto the world. This expansive love then becomes the foundation upon which many relationships can be built simultaneously. The couple's union will enable them to offer a refuge, like an island in the Pacific Ocean welcoming all to sit and rest a while. This island is stable because the two souls who created it have evolved to know that love is truly all encompassing and extends, rather than takes. Their deep love sees and protects each partner's *inherited innocence,*[2] rather than projecting guilt. All decisions and actions that both partners take are rooted in the awareness of the truth of their eternal being. The couple acknowledges that while mistakes are unavoidable, they can also be seen as opportunities to love oneself and the other even more deeply. A couple whose partnership is built upon the new marriage paradigm will have learned that the true love they offer each other transcends all of their fears of loss and abandonment, rejection, and

---

[2] Our innocence is implied and protected because we were created out of perfect love, and that attribute is constant.

unworthiness—their love is stable, constant, and un-encumbered.

The couple in the new marriage paradigm will already be correcting the false idea that in order to have, one needs to keep. Instead, they will be unified in their goal and understand that what they give, they will actually have more of. It is for this reason that the mutual protection of each other's innocence is so crucial to the ongoing success of their partnership.

The framework of the new marriage paradigm invites couples to powerful realizations that facilitate a more loving relationship. Specifically, there is the awareness that each partner has, in fact, married someone similar to either their mother or father, in order to grow in self-love and appreciation. Each person will pursue and marry someone who reflects the traits of the parent by whom they perceive it was most difficult to feel accepted, approved of, and valued.

In truth, the perceived emotionally estranged parent is seen to embody the traits that the soul is learning to love within him- or herself. Our parents are just reflections of the two sides of our all-encompassing natures that we own and value, disown and deny.

Because every person will ultimately be attracted to, and then couple with, the primary personality traits of either their mother or father—the parent they felt most rejected by—the dance of marriage is destined to heal and integrate the personalities of each soul. It does so as the soul heals perceived hurts from childhood rejection or trauma that are un-consciously running the relationships in which the soul is engaged. In this book, we will also explore how in our marriages we unconsciously adopt parent/child roles that are embraced in order to control our mates, and which, if not abandoned, will inevitably destroy intimacy for the couple. This will be discussed at length in chapter five, entitled *Why We Marry "Our Parents."*

As a longtime student and teacher of *A Course in Miracles* (a self-study discipline aimed at correcting the false belief of our separation from our creator, also referred to as "the Course"), I now invite you to join with me in upholding the new marriage paradigm. It is my sincerest wish that, as a result of reading this book, your marriage will be strengthened or lovingly surrendered if that is the best option for you and your spouse. The surrender of the relationship becomes necessary only when one of the mates is unwilling to grow. Listen carefully to your deeply questioning heart, and trust its wisdom.

Chapter One

Why We Marry

People marry to accomplish differing goals. These goals and achievements, as well as acquirements, are often driven by the partners' desires and values. For instance, Bob and Cathy, who are in their late twenties, are both schoolteachers. They met four years ago, have dated seriously for the past 18 months, and are engaged to be married. They both want children soon, and they want to have summers off together to spend at Cathy's parents' cabin, just as her parents did when she was little.

They share the dream of wanting to raise a tight-knit family, and both feel valued and appreciated because their common primary desires weave a bond between them. Cathy and Bob also enjoy outdoor sports and spend many weekends hiking. Their relationship allows them to pursue their highest values together.

Throughout their marriage, there will be a hierarchy of perceived voids, which will, in turn, drive their values, such as more children, financial freedom, a business partnership, deepened friendship, a more fiery sexual companionship, and so on.

As each void becomes filled, a new desire will follow, and those desires will often be reflective of the changes that affect them as they age, mature, and evolve soulfully.

Individually and as a couple, as they move from void to void and acquire what they pursue, a new set of desires will rush in to meet them. Through continued acquisitions, they will grow in their sense of power.

Sometimes the new void that we perceive as a value to acquire, such as financial freedom, will require skills and drive that our current partner does not have, nor will want to attain. When the people we are with do not wish to pursue our primary values with us, and especially if they are against our pursuit of these values, the relationship will begin to become strained and, in time, will likely end. When this dynamic occurs, we will begin to pursue others who value what we value at that particular stage in our life. Therefore, the reason for the next union may well be different from the one that drove the previous relationship.

In twenty years, Bob and Cathy may be pursuing spirituality, their own business, financial freedom, travel, or retirement. If one of them perceives that the other does not put sufficient energy into the pursuit of one or more of these values, then they may well be attracted to another mate who they feel is more in alignment with their values at that time. A more detailed explanation of values and their roles in a relationship is provided in chapter six.

As indicated, the reasons for getting married vary, but there are a few common driving forces we should review. Interestingly, because perceived voids are always present, some of the key reasons we unite are associated with fear and loss, yet aren't always in our conscious awareness.

Love and Fear

On a deeper level, we are afraid that no one else will love us. We might marry due to pregnancy and our unwillingness to raise a child alone. We unite because we are afraid of being lonely and of growing old alone. We take the plunge because we are afraid of what our family and peers will think about our remaining unwed—the "what-is-wrong-with-us" question. We say "I do" because we are afraid of hurting our partner, even if we've changed our mind about the relationship. We commit because we are afraid of financial insecurity. And we settle with a partner, wondering if this person is really the best we can do, while being terrified of finding out the answer. Take some time now to review which, if any, of these reasons applied in your original decision to marry.

As a therapist specializing in marriage counseling, I have tallied that 70 percent of couples married for reasons that are among those listed above. I believe it would be helpful for you to be aware of those reasons, yet not feel guilty for them.

On the other hand, we also marry because we are very much in love and are ready to embark on the "roller coaster" of marriage. We couple because we are prepared to change and grow with one another. We are willing, over the years, to unveil the layers blocking acts of intimacy and vulnerability that we once were terrified of facing. We want to raise a family and grow old together—a dream that many newlyweds begin with. So, why do we only have a 50 percent chance of accomplishing that goal?

The reasons we separate and divorce vary, and will be discussed at length in chapter two. However, one of the most crippling components in a relationship is our failure to communicate openly and honestly with one another. This is so, because in not communicating, we are saying that we want to remain separate and hidden.

Communicating Truthfully

Communication is achieved by knowing our needs and ourselves and feeling safe to share those needs and discoveries with our partner. To communicate means to love, because it is an act of union. Yet, communication is not just verbal; it is an emotional, mental, physical, and spiritual act that joins us to one another. The soul is highly vested in partnership because we can discover our deeper nature, our healed and unhealed selves. Secretly, we pray that our partner will not recoil in horror when faced with our fractures. When they do not, we feel deeply connected because we are able to touch the innocence that lies beneath our perceived guilt and shame. Guilt and shame are rooted deeply within our unconscious as a result of the hidden desires we have been too afraid to express, and the past mistakes we think we have made, and which we don't want our partner to know about. Guilty feelings also arise from keeping secret the real reasons we married. Through communicating our discoveries, fears, and inspirations, we bond. When we can share those discoveries without being judged, we feel valued and loved as we are.

Security and Ideals

Let's take some time now to look more closely at the "security" reasons we marry. I was seventeen the first time I said "I do," and I was seven months pregnant with another man's child. I married a young man whom I was certain I could "love back to emotional health." I knew that he had deeply seated emotional hurts and feelings of having been rejected by his parents, and I decided I could "fix" them. In my heart, I knew that he did not love me, but that he had a set of ideals that he was able to uphold through becoming my husband.

These ideals included upholding his parents' beliefs about living together, and embracing their idea that getting a girl pregnant was sinful. (Of course, his parents could not conceive of the fact that he would be with a girl who was pregnant with another guy's child.) The primary ideal he bought into was that it was a sin to live with someone you wouldn't marry. He was deeply torn between getting parental approval, his heart's yearning to be with his first love who had broken up with him a year prior to our encounter, and his wish to have a son to whom he could be the dad that he felt his father never was. I gave birth to a baby girl.

I married him because I ached to be wanted, even if it was just minimally. I was a "fixer" and wanted to prove my inner wisdom on the power of love to him. I truly believed that my love was special and that I could heal him. I wanted to make him happy and to prove my worthiness above all else. I was not afraid of being a single parent because my mother had raised me and my brothers on her own after my father left when I was seven years old—and so I felt comfortable with such a scenario.

Each of us had a very different set of goals that our union was to achieve. The marriage stability was reflective of our independent goals being met. In my birthing a girl and not a boy, I jeopardized an already fragile union. As my husband's former love showed a renewed interest in him, our marriage became further cracked. My in-laws were playing roulette with my future with every supportive or challenging visit. After four-and-a-half years of living in a tumultuous marriage, which produced two daughters, we separated. He had found his soulmate, who bore him a son within a year of their union. Our marriage ended.[3]

The primary reason we marry is that we want to share and expand our life. We want to see the Grand Canyon, Pantheon, or Eiffel Tower, with someone we cherish. We want to be with a mate to pass on our genetic seed, and do the challenging task of raising a family. We want to care and be cared for. We want to feel respected, loved, valued, and irreplaceable. Somehow we just know that lifting a weight with a friend makes that weight more manageable. Inherently, we know that life will challenge our soul

---

[3] The details of this relationship are described in my autobiography, *Our Cosmic Dance.*

and personality, and so we want to share the burden. Ultimately, we want to be happy, and we seem to be genetically programmed to couple in order to experience a very specific form of joy.

In every house of marriage,
there's room for an interpreter.

Stanley Kunitz

Chapter Two

Why We Divorce

Divorce can be driven by one of two implementers. One is the ego and its need for an exclusive relationship, and the second is the spirit and its desire to continue its growth through soulful love. When splitting up is driven by the ego, a great deal of pain will be a part of the experience, because by the ego's standards, the exclusivity, which is based on lack, is being thwarted. However, when spirit prompts the decision, a great deal of love and appreciation will be choreographed into the last dance the pair shares as partners.

The fundamental difference between these two initiators is the foundation on which the need for separation was built. For the spirit, divorce is really an impossibility, since it knows that all relationships are eternal because of the love that inspired them and was created within them. Further, the spirit knows that we cannot divorce ourselves, and since we are a part of a collective being, we are in truth just moving towards another part of ourselves that will be reflected by a new mate. Therefore, the spirit will evaluate divorce as being a restructuring of the relationship dynamics between the couple. The spirit will know that what the two souls came together to learn has been accomplished. Each soul will, with a deep sense of completion and gratitude, give thanks to the other for the love that was extended and integrated through their union. The couple will have deepened their capacity to be intimate, honest, and transparent, and ultimately will have grown in self-love.

Each will have gained in appreciation of their own brilliance through loving the parts of themselves they once perceived as unlovable. Both souls will cherish the time spent together and will protect it from guilt. From the spirit's perspective, the experience of divorce can be joyful because it knows that the relationship will continue, albeit in a different form. Lastly, each individual will still offer the other an opportunity to expand their soul through friendship and caring because of the journey they shared and their joint accomplishments.

Ego Nudgings

One of the reasons the ego wants divorce may be that we were embracing love by protecting innocence, rather than guilt, in ourselves and the other. The protection of innocence is an outrage to the ego. We may well be under the illusion that if both partners live the Course principles, their marriage is secure. This is not always so. The ego will kick in and fight even as we live more soulfully.

Alternatively, we may be releasing guilt and recognizing that there is no lack of any kind in either of the mates. The ego cannot tolerate the recognition of these truths. Consequently, if one or both partners are no longer willing to be the scapegoat for the guilt that has been projected onto them, the natural outcome will seem to be divorce. Another reason we may not want to stay married is because we no longer wish to connect the drives and values of our mate to our own (see chapter six, *How Values Drive Relationships*).

Since we all pair initially because we see in another something valuable that we do not perceive to have in us, the acquiring of this "thing" becomes the driving force sustaining the relationship. Once we have acquired the "thing," the ego whispers, "Find something else to take, or leave." In the ego's evaluation, a reason that justifies divorce is when your mate is no longer willing to fill a perceived lack or need in you that they had previously agreed to fill.

Both egos will stay engaged within a relationship for as long as their "special love" can be sustained. The word "special" entails that the partners have agreed to shelter each other from guilt by perceiving it in everyone other than themselves. Each has a silent agreement to provide for the other "something," such as financial security, housekeeping, parenthood, accountability or the lack thereof, rescuing, or companionship, which the giver has convinced the taker they can't provide for themselves. Finally, the last dominant component seen in the special relationship dynamic is that each ego is really trying to take away some perceived asset that the mate has. Once the individual has secured the asset that they perceived as being unavailable to them through any other tactic, they will leave.[4]

The whispers of the ego are thus, "You are not worth anything, nor have anything of value in your nature...if anyone saw you for who you really are, they would recoil in horror...therefore take what you can quickly...and then run and hide what you have stolen from your mate before they can see what you have done."

Each partner will initially be driven by a perceived void, and each will feel very grateful to anyone who appears to be covering it. The mate cannot really fill the lack because the truth is that lack does not exist. If this truth is brought to awareness, anger and fear usually rush to the surface, as the mate then feels conned, and quickly blames the spouse for the betrayal. It is for all the aforementioned reasons that the special love relationship is founded on lack, robbery, and exclusion.

The Authentic Voice of Spirit

Spirit, on the other hand, can and will nudge for the completion of a relationship because the two souls have accomplished what they came together to do. These accomplishments will include integrating unloved parts of themselves, nurturing and acquiring full independence in a specific area, or all areas, of the mate's life, or because they have a dance to do with another soul who is contracted to take them to the

---

[4] For detailed information regarding the ego and the special relationship dynamic, please see my book *Rediscovering Your Authentic Self*.

next level of integration, intimacy, transparency, and authentic power. Another possible reason might be that one partner is choosing a direction for their life that appears incongruent with that of their mate. What is certain is that if spirit initiates the separation or divorce, the journey will be gentle and all words and actions will be filtered through the golden rule: I shall do unto you only what I would have done unto me. And I am certain that I have loved you fully, accepting and appreciating you as you are.

Some relationships end long before the divorce begins. One or both souls have awoken to the authentic self's desire to be more intimate and transparent—in short, more real. When the ego is aroused to this inevitable desire, we meet a crossroads in the marriage, and an invitation to love more deeply will be extended. At this point, we will decide to deepen or lessen our heart's capacity to love. The importance of this decision, and how to open rather than harden our heart, will be explored in depth in the next chapter.

The Importance of Feeling Valued

Lastly, the reasons for leaving a marriage may simply be that we do not believe that our mate values what we do, and thus we feel unloved. In this dynamic, we are oblivious to the understanding that we are, in fact, more committed to meeting our needs than we are committed to our spouse. The hard truth is that we are always in pursuit of what we feel is missing and perceive to be of great importance and, sadly, value even more than we value each other. In fact, our commitment to our mate is directly influenced by our perception of how they help us get what we desire. The key to unlocking the door of communication is knowing how to get each other talking by asking questions of our spouse in the areas that are important to them. In this way, we will learn how to make each other feel valued and appreciated, as we recognize the equality of the needs of both souls.

In every marriage
more than a week old,
there are grounds for divorce.
The trick is to find
grounds for marriage.

Robert Anderson,
Solitaire & Double Solitaire

Chapter Three

The New vs. the Old Paradigm of Marriage

The foundation on which the new marriage paradigm is built is primarily one in which both partners realize that they are whole and complete in and of themselves—they don't depend on each other to complete their lives. The word "marriage" does not necessarily mean that a couple signs a legal marriage contract, but rather that both partners have paralleled their lives and wish to support each other's soul expression and the dreams encompassed by it.

Soulful individuals do not unite out of a perceived lack or need, nor are they interested in projecting guilt onto each other for mistakes that each will make along the way. Both souls are well aware that they have come together to learn what traits they perceive in each other that prompt them to shut their hearts to love. These traits include the beliefs they hold that each partner sees to be detrimental to their advancement as a couple, e.g., selfishness, grumpiness, dishonesty. Each individual has formulated an ideal of what they want to have. When one of the parties challenges that ideal, the challenge becomes a "block" to their ability to feel and experience love. Most importantly, the couple acknowledges that they have joined in order to identify and then remove all the blocks that prevent them from giving and receiving unconditional love and appreciation.

Soul-Filled Love

In the new paradigm, the partners have come together to share their fullness, and to co-create opportunities for joint growth. In addition, both souls are aware that the relationship facilitates dynamics to expose and heal each of their memories of being rejected and wounded by a previous mate. And it is understood that the wounds that emerge have engaged *defensive coping mechanisms*, which the ego (the inauthentic self) employs to protect its interests and sustain the desire for separation and guilt.

In a soulful relationship, the partners understand that they have joined together to heal their wounds from the past by letting the "now" take precedence over the past. In doing so, they are able to be mirrors for each other *now,* and expose the parts of themselves that were once believed to be shameful and unlovable. As both souls recognize within themselves, and then take ownership of, the same shadowed traits they see in the other, they are able to advance in soul-filled love, thus co-creating the new marriage paradigm.

In the old marriage paradigm, the ego will work diligently to have the wounded party believe that the *past* hurt is what gives the soul permission to protect it *now.* This defensive stance is what projection is founded upon. Projection happens whenever we mix an unloved trait that we want to hide and deny within ourselves with an unloved memory that we then project out onto a new situation. It is as if we had a blank canvas from which all pictures have been erased and, instead of creating a new picture, we paint the old picture back onto the canvas. Interestingly, we then feel confused as to why we keep having the same problems in our relationships. Therefore, the new paradigm is geared towards undoing projection and instead nurturing both souls towards the opportunity to paint a new picture, thus facilitating the understanding and eventual healing of what was once misunderstood.

With projection, the assumption is that what happened in the past *must* happen now. This is so because the part of the mind that does the thinking is the part that still believes and worships "specialness," the past, guilt, and autonomy. It is the part of the mind that is asleep to its true unifying self as it is *now*. A key difference, then, between those living in the special vs. the soulful relationship is that the latter operates in the *now*.

The souls that have made the decision to transform their relationship or marriage into the new paradigm will first need to recognize the key differences in each model. As mentioned in chapter one, marriage contracts in the past were signed for many reasons, but primarily for security—be it emotional, psycho-logical, or financial.

We married in order to have a family or a "tribe," and to share our life with another soul who we hoped would take our side in our fight *against the world*. In fact, the ego uses the union as a way to separate the couple from the world. This is true because the ego itself is an outpicturing of the desire for "specialness" and autonomy, which results in exclusion. The original desire of the ego is that each of us stands individually against the world, but as the ego hears our inherent and insatiable request to be unified with someone, as we were in our creation, it compromises and allows a union to occur with another individual, provided that the couple now work together against the world.

The desire to be autonomous is incongruous with our true nature because we are really a part of a much greater whole. Since we forget our wholeness, we feel a need for protective and defensive action, so that we are able to uphold our ego selves. But each time we fully join with another in heart and mind, the ego "evaporates."

Expansive and Inclusive Love

In the new paradigm, the soulful relationship is inclusive of the couple, their families, and the rest of the world. Neither of the souls wishes to exclude others because each has come to understand that all people are reflections of them, and thus offer the opportunity for growth, a more expansive love, peace of mind, brotherhood, and spiritual advancement.

In soulful love relationships, we understand that each of the individuals is inherently innocent. This innocence does not come from any actions in which they participate or the absence thereof, but rather it reflects their natural identity before it is blocked by fear (the belief in separation) of some kind. It is understood between the souls that all fear is ultimately connected to a perceived potential loss, and that all correction of that perception comes from questioning why we feel we need something or someone other than our authentic identity.

The truth about us is that we are in need of nothing. We are powerful, radiant, and abundant beings. Therefore, when we are aligned with that truth and our beliefs reflect that as well, love rather than fear prevails in the relationship. Furthermore, this means that the souls' rather than the egos' personas are upheld as the true partners engaged in the dance.

It should be noted that the result of questioning anything that is associated with lack or loss usually leaves the fear exposed, and the individual can recognize that it is indeed based on ego rather than spirit identification. Since the couple is in pursuit of a soulful rather than a special relationship, whenever either party discovers a perceived loss or lack, they share their findings and work in tandem to undo the belief. This soul-searching work magnifies for us that the "who" (either ego or spirit) drives the "what" (innocence/truth or guilt/illusion) through which the relationship is upheld.

To recapitulate the points stated above, the ego uses relationships to project and hide the guilt that we will ultimately feel inside, because the ego has hypnotized us into thinking that we are something we are not, namely a body. Since the body is what the ego identifies with and would have us believe we are, and its identity is dependent upon our believing it, the ego must make us feel afraid and confused, so that it can protect us against the truth. In our allowing it to do so, however, we lose sight of our true selves as spirit and love, and instead believe that we are limited and confined to a death sentence because we consider ourselves to be a body.

In our confusion, we actually relinquish our ability to be the decision-maker. It is like the cartoon in which the character stands with a little devil on one shoulder and an angel on the other. The character becomes the decision-maker in the question of which self will lead, and depending on which is chosen, the actions and outcomes will lead to peace or conflict, truth or illusion. The confusion over what we identify with, and the deep inner knowing that we are not in alignment with our authentic selves, causes us to question everything. Consequently, we feel alone and are on a very deep level terrified of being found out, by anyone including our mate, for this lie we are living. Since we associate the revealing of a lie that we have told with embarrassment and shame, we work diligently against such an exposure, and in doing so, actually work against our own greater good, and soulful relationships. It is for this reason that the special relationship is said to be the substitute for our real relationship with love, our authentic self, or the divine.

Cause and Effect

Most of us at times think that we are at the effect, rather than the cause, of our life. In particular, we are prone to such reversals within the dynamics of our romantic relationship. We forget, or have never been taught, that we are quite literally living out what our core beliefs are about ourselves, each other, and the world.

Often, we are oblivious to the fact that the way we treat ourselves is reflected back to us by our mate. The *self* we establish in our relationships will indeed attract very different dances with varying dance partners. This is so because the foundations and beliefs held by each of these opposing selves are so different. So, if we are under the belief that we are unlovable, guilty, deprived, broken, and shadowed, we will attract behaviors from our partner to reflect those beliefs back to us. Consequently, when we are realigned with our true selves, we attract that which is congruent with our deeper and authentic identity as being abundant, lovable, innocent, charitable, compassionate, and so on. This transfer of identification is itself the shift from special to soulful relationships—the transformation from the old into the new paradigm of marriage.

In the soulful relationship dynamic, we realize that we *create, attract, or become anything we have not learned to love;* relationships can, therefore, be at times very painful. From this recognition, however, we can learn to understand and appreciate a disliked trait or action in another or in us and to recognize how it facilitates greatness, growth, and opportunity. When we do so, we turn "rejection" into appreciation, which opens the heart to loving and appreciating all of each other and ourselves more fully, and this is congruent with the new marriage paradigm. With this understanding, our relationships become transformative models for potential soul growth and development.

The traits and qualities we do not love and understand are usually driven by our limited awareness of how what we evaluate as negative simultaneously unfolds the positive. For instance, the perceived stinginess of my mate will initiate my generosity. Further, my evaluation of this trait in him will invite me to see and love it in myself. Although I may perceive him to be stingy in offering up his time, I may realize that I am stingy with lending out my books. As I am wise enough to realize that fear is driving this trait in me and in him, I can decide to realign my belief, making it congruent with my real and abundant self. Once I have done so, I will have a new *self* which he can "mirror" back to me.

In this model of growth, you will notice that I did not ask him to change in any way, nor was it necessary for me to do so. Instead, I owned that same trait (stinginess) within myself and integrated it into my deeper nature. This integration process is what nurtures us to be who or what we really are.

Defensiveness is the most common indicator that ego, rather than spirit, is directing the relationship and the issues between partners. Defensiveness is a sure sign that cause and effect have been split and reversed. The splitting means that we believe there is a time lag, which establishes a space between what we think and how we experience that thought. This is an illusion the ego cherishes, because it keeps us "at effect" and powerless to change our lives and relationships.

When we are in contact with our authentic self, we feel safe, secure, open-hearted, open-minded, and empowered to communicate, rather than dictate, our needs and desires. If communication means that we can both speak and hear one another, and thus recognize each other's perceptions and work collectively to find common ground between the parties, then communication becomes an expression of love. Since "special relationships" are not based on love, but rather are based on fear because of the association with separation, the lack of communication that emerges is understandable.

To know that each soul is cause in the relationship, and to be certain that each is in a three-dimensional experience of their core beliefs, is truly freeing. In this model, we are free and empowered to co-create any relationship we feel will serve our goal. If we are true to our authentic selves, our goal will be love.

There are two ways of spreading light:
to be the candle
or the mirror that reflects it.

Edith Wharton

Chapter Four

Chemistry, Fire, and Intimacy

Chemistry, fire, and passion are feelings we all experience at some point in our lives. When we are under their intoxicating influence, we feel powerful, beautiful, loved, valued, and appreciated. They are the magic potion awakening us to potential love and hopes for procreation and can be elicited at the onset of a new relationship and the synonymous exploration of another soul that we are interested in mating with. It should be noted that either a person or an inspiring idea could invoke passion. However, for the purposes of this book, we will direct our attention towards romantically focused relationships.

Many of us have been hypnotized into the belief that chemistry *must* be a key ingredient in our initial pursuit of a lasting romantic relationship. I do not believe this to be true. When I first met Allan, my husband of ten years, I did not feel chemistry towards him, although I had great admiration, respect, and friendship for him.

I'll admit that I eventually began yearning for the "high" that chemical attraction brings, and which had been a component of all my previous romantic encounters. It had become dormant within me. After almost ten years of marriage, the desire for fire reemerged within me and thus within our relationship.

We had experienced a highly intense yet short interlude with fire and the insatiable yearning to melt into one another following a two-month separation a year after we began dating. The acts of intimacy we engaged in during that time encompassed every level of our being—spiritual, emotional, intellectual. For me, the intense fire lasted about six months, after which it slowly subsided until only sparks and flickers remained about a year later. As chemically ignited flames began to flicker and burn out, our love simultaneously began to deepen and become much less confining and possessive.

Over the years, we've discussed divorce openly and as frequently as each of us was considering it, usually following a period of stress directly connected to the raising of my children from previous marriages. For each of us, the discussion about separation or divorce was without fear, since it was not used as a tool of manipulation, but rather as a frank and directive option we were at times flirting with.

The primary hurdle we needed to stride over was the intensely multifaceted work of blending families, coupled with my fast-growing career and my unavailability to be the primary care-giving parent I had once been. I believe that these lifestyle "ingredients" were vital to both the emergence and the extinguishing of fire.

When my desire for fire reemerged (Allan's had never been extinguished), I began my deeper search for understanding of why it emerged at that particular time. More specifically, it was of particular interest for me to discover that the yearning for fire did not resurface until our relationship had matured and our children had left home. I believed that these were foundations that could breathe oxygen onto embers and again produce fire.

From my personal experience, a more meaningful question would be to ask whether chemistry is really needed to create a mature loving and sharing relationship. And if so, when it seems to be dormant, is it really? Or is fire actually present, yet burning in a different arena of life at different times of our relationship?

I believed the latter to be true, and realized that my marriage demonstrated this. I have come to realize that even chemistry and fire can and do have more and less appropriate times to be ignited, in particular places. In this chapter, we will explore my discoveries.

Lastly, I wanted to investigate why we feel fire towards some individuals and not others, and what, if any, are the benefits and potential drawbacks of chemistry or fire, and whether it is necessary at all to have fire within a relationship to have a fulfilling, soulful love dance with another person.

Encountering Fire

My first memory of an encounter with this mysterious potion we call chemistry stems from the time I was in grade two of elementary school. I was deeply attracted to Jeffrey, who was my classmate and about whom I felt that everything was perfect. Most of all, I adored Jeffrey's gorgeous brown eyes and olive-colored skin—he was Asian. Whenever I was around him, I felt as though I could do anything, and as if I were the most beautiful girl in the world. I felt powerful, important, and my self-esteem soared.

To have such powerful feelings of self-approval from being with another soul whom I evaluated as being equally magical as I felt when I was in his presence seemed indeed miraculous. What I felt when I was near him acknowledged that the dance of romantic relationships and, in particular, an encounter igniting vulnerability, was attractive, bliss-filled, and intoxicating. Memories of these powerful feelings conjure up an absolute certainty of how we must feel when we are aware of our uninterruptible union with the divine. In this sense, unbridled love between souls is the reflection of our union with God. Is it any wonder, therefore, that we pursue it with such determination?

Whenever two souls have the courage to merge, it is a dance between the lover and the beloved, where, for a moment, each sees in the other only their respective perfection and radiance. As a child, I never understood this. The reason I felt so good and so lovable when Jeffrey smiled at me was not important—only receiving his approval was. In the moment I had his approval, Jeffrey became a surrogate for the divine. Unknowingly, Jeffrey ignited within me an ancient soul memory of the approval, love, and gratitude that my Creator felt not only for me, but for each and every one of us. And although I could never have intellectualized this concept at the time, it is transparently clear to me now that falling in love with other souls here on earth is the counterpart to our being in love with God, even though we may not usually be aware of this.

As a child, I did not understand the impact that my perceived ideals of a great mate could have on my body, nor did I consciously need to know the recipe of the magic concoction of hormones which, when blended together in perfect proportions, released feelings of sexual arousal, ecstasy, and omnipotence within my body. Nevertheless, all the feelings of intoxication and bliss were somehow the by-product of Jeffrey's approval, acceptance, and attention.

Then there was Stephen; he, too, was in my grade-two classroom. He was cute, funny, and clearly attracted to me. Strangely enough, though, with Stephen, there were only feelings of "brotherhood" that emerged whenever he looked at me.

The reasons why I had such different feelings for these two boys are complex and are based on an interesting mixture of both the function of the animal part of my brain and the emotional/psychological desires I held, and still hold. This phenomenon will be explored at length in the next section. Stephen was a great-looking little boy, who felt fire towards me, so why was it not transferable? Why was his approval of me not important in my mind? What was it he had, or in my perception did not have, that created feelings of brotherhood rather than passion and desire? I wanted to know!

The Chemistry of Passionate Love

What causes chemistry, passion, and the deep sexual attraction I like to call *fire* between some people? And why does it emerge with some and not with others? Why does it emerge at times with an individual and then disappear? I desperately needed answers to these key questions, not only for the clients I counseled, but also for myself as a deeply devoted wife, who had somehow misplaced or covered the fire she once felt. I suspected that one of the many factors that had snuffed out the flames was my pursuit of other priorities. Another key factor could have been the past hurts or resentments that I had avoided discussing and healing through meaningful communication. And the most crippling force could have been a personality trait that I coveted more than fire—autonomy.

Through hours of investigation into the components of chemistry, I discovered that what arouses the fire in us is made up of intricate measures of fantasy and illusion—the hidden and exposed parts of each other and ourselves. The ingredients are both the known and the unknown, the familiar and the mystery, and the physical attributes of our parents. The predominant aspects and traits of the individual to whom we feel chemically attracted include the physical (overall look, scent, ethnic orientation, height, weight, and hair color), the emotional (mysterious, impartial, warm, kind, gentle, nurturing, cool, mean, aloof), and the overall psychological and personality makeup (street-smart, witty, diligent, hard-working, intelligent, funny, committed, unfaithful, intimidator, control freak, princess, warrior, knight, mother, etc.) that remind us of who we are in our "light," not shadowed, side.

In addition, the individual to whom we feel attracted is the embodiment of the person we *wished* we could have had as a parental figure. In short, this fantasized figure is the culmination of the primarily valued and appreciated traits of our mother and father, without their shadow sides. So, we want the two positive sides, including the physical features of mom and dad, to be a single individual, and when we believe that we have found that personified soul, we feel fire! I believe that in "finding" them, we finally feel secure enough to be all that we are, and to express our fullest nature, which encompasses both vulnerability and confidence. The traits and qualities that we perceive as "proof" that we were, and still are, worthy of being loved and approved of, concurrently elicit sparks. Since this idealized figure is a fantasy, the sparks will eventually fade with this realization, hopefully into a deeper love that is more truthful and reflective of the holistic nature of our parents and, ultimately, of us.

For example, I am most attracted to the physical attributes of my father in men, and conversely most attracted to the moral, playful, flirtatious, and spiritual virtues of my mother. If I perceive a man to encompass the embodiment of both my parents, then my heart stops and my head turns to follow this person, almost without my conscious awareness. In the moments I see the dream figure, whether I know them or not, I am consumed. In that moment, the young emotional "I" feels fully accepted and safe. In time, however, the little girl with perceived unmet needs will have to mature into a woman, as she works with a mate to fill those needs. It is the dance between juicy fire and a deeper integrated self that keeps the relationship alive.

I have concluded that what is happening in my mind when I see the fantasized man is that I am only seeing one half of them—the half that I have equated with pleasure, comfort, safety, fun, and feeling in control.

These ingredients make up half of the chemical mixture necessary to create fire. The second part of the chemical mixture we need for fire will be pursued and evaluated, albeit at lightning speed, and will involve a dance of power and control.

For me, the displacement of fiery passion, which had been a common bedfellow of mine ever since I can remember, happened gradually over the years. And, as mentioned earlier, as the fire dwindled, a deeper, more enriched love based on respect seemed to fill the space that sexual passion once occupied. Still, my question was, can I have both? Is it not possible to have a deeply mature and enduring love coupled with an insatiable hunger for sexual intimacy and a deep fulfillment of that burning desire? I hoped that our souls and our love had grown to a level that could envelop both. I needed to discover the answers to these powerful questions.

The Quest for Power and Control

So, as had happened so many times before, my life and my own marriage became the primary workbook for learning about the reasons why we love and fall out of love—the reasons we find and misplace passion and lose sight of why we love altogether, when other things take the front seat in our list of wishes and desires. I needed to discover why I had a spark for Allan, but not the fire I yearned to have with him again. My quest was to uncover what was suffocating the oxygen from the spark, which I so deeply wanted to turn into a blaze. In my heart I knew that, if I was to be truly and fully satisfied with our relationship, I needed to have it all!

Long hours of introspection revealed that, on some level, we were engaged in a deeply entrenched power struggle to maintain control. I inquired as to how and why we distanced ourselves from one another in certain situations, or when discussing certain topics. I concluded that there was some element or issue related to our individual need for power and control that needed to be addressed. Understanding that all problems start at the thought level, I searched my mind for what ideas I may have been entertaining that were not in alignment with my goal of passion for Allan. Each of us had been holding a hidden belief that was acting as the culprit of our demise. Recognizing that beliefs have power only if we fuel them with our acknowledgment, I realized I had full control of changing them—once I knew what they were.

It was a "belief" or an "idea," likely untrue, that was extinguishing the passion between us. Therefore, I needed to explore my deepest beliefs and desires to unearth and then disable this idea.

Since all souls attract other souls primarily because they are mirrors for each other, I knew that Allan must be holding the same belief, although it may be showing up in a different form for him. The form, so to speak, would be reflective of one of the things he valued most. The same was true for me. My search then became directive in that I needed to focus on what he and I valued and viewed as our individual powers. The pursuit and management of whatever we perceived as powerful were integral for each of us to maintain individual control over the other. This particular tool of power, which can be a trait, physical object, position, role, or title, gains its influence in our minds because we believe that we can control others with it. These types of beliefs are often socially fuelled, and we have unconsciously bought into them. Examples of such beliefs are "beauty is power" and "financial independence creates more freedom."

Being fully aware of this, I began my journey to uncover Allan's fear-ridden belief, as well as my own. I had known for years that we were engaged in an unconscious power struggle, but up until I began to look for fire, I had not felt the need to deal with it. In my heart, I knew we each had held back a little something in hopes of maintaining an ounce more power than the other had. We did this unconsciously, to secure our position and control in the relationship. In short, we were afraid of equality and, in particular, of intimacy—the melting in of our protective boundaries. Therefore, we withheld parts of ourselves and some of our acquisitions, to protect ourselves from being totally vulnerable.

Next, I examined another fact that I had uncovered as a therapist and marriage counselor. I reviewed something else that typically happens in long-term love relationships: We are propelled to eventually either deepen the level of intimacy, or go numb. As we grow in soul strength, meaning we become more and more integrated as a whole being, we become less fearful in our ability to admit that we are simultaneously strong and powerless with one another. We begin to become more reliant on spiritual or internal strength (authentic power) and less interested in material or external force (pseudo power). In light of this, we reshape our relationships and their objectives. With each advance of the individual parties comes a shifting or reassigning of what is perceived to be the new "power tool" to maintain control in the relationship. Remember, control is a primary arsenal of the ego, and it directs us vigilantly to keep it at all costs!

Romantic relationships are largely driven by ego dynamics—the desire for a "special relationship." I would like to remind you that "special relationship" means a relationship that is autonomous, exclusive, and different, regardless of whether that difference is seen as making the relationship better or worse than any other relationship. "Special" always equals some sense of exclusion and control, which the ego equates with power, because it rules another instead of merging with them as an equal. Since we cannot reach intimacy without a merger of being, fire in this framework is unattainable.

As Allan and I grew in our understanding of love, or, to say it differently, as we grew in our spiritual connectedness with God, we simultaneously felt less and less possessive of each other. The ego sensed this foundational change, and directed us thus, "Any movement in the direction of love (God) is threatening to us (our special relationship) and should be protected against." It is true that soulful love, and any movement towards it, is an assault on the ego. It is equally true, however, that authentic love is not threatening to our true self or a soulful relationship. In short, Allan and I were being attracted to a place of decision—a crossroads with diametrically opposed outcomes.

One path was that of the spirit, a gently posed passageway towards divine love, which is treed with innocence and pardon, equality and union, while the other was governed by the ego—the false sense of self we covet. This was a wide and well-paved road, supported with boulders of guilt, exclusion, possession, and fear. Allan and I chose the road less traveled—the road of love and freedom, and one that fosters the desire to live in the moment.

In turn, our egos' response to our decision was to submerge our prized protective "tool" even deeper into our unconscious. Each ego masterfully protected against our soulful decision and joint willingness to repeatedly choose the path that would uphold our freedom to leave the relationship at any time we felt that we had completed what we had joined to do.

Consequently, each of us was symbolically holding an "ace," which was viewed as our dearest treasure, but by then, it was buried deeply beyond our immediate reach.

The ego was now positioned as a skillful card player, determined to win. And as any good card player knows, we are not willing to reveal this power card unless we have to! The ace would not be revealed to the mate unless there was a potential to lose something we evaluated as being even dearer than the ace.

Since our souls were committed only to revealing our deeper soulful love, a "something" had to emerge to entice us to commit to a total surrender of love, and each other. That something was intimacy and transparency.

If indeed fear is the dragon that guards our deepest treasure, then we needed to find the gift in slaying this fear-filled belief for ourselves, and to attain our next level of soulful union. And so, together, we prepared to embark upon that journey.

The ultimate act of intimacy and vulnerability would be in exposing and offering that treasured ace to each other. To reveal our ace was a fundamental requirement if we were going to take our marriage into the new paradigm, where it would be based on transparency, freedom, partnership, appreciation, equality, empowerment, non-attachment, and total commitment to ourselves as equally as to each other.

I wanted this model of marriage more than anything else, and I decided that I would leave no stone unturned to establish its key components and then nurture the necessary ingredients to sustain it. I was committed to the partnership's full capacity to reveal our individual and partnered brilliance. I wanted this level of love, not so that I could be guaranteed a lifelong marriage with Allan, but rather so that I would know we had a marriage partnership that facilitated total soul advancement and the revealing of anything that had once blocked our fullest expression of love.

Allan and I had been together for nearly ten years, and he had met my most valued needs, such as friendship, intellectual stimulus, similar moral values, shared parenthood, financial security, and, over time, he had even become my spiritual partner. For almost ten years, the fulfillment of these roles was enough for me. In fact, as I looked back, I realized that I had wanted God more than I had wanted fire in our relationship, and in fact, had there been fire, it may well have impeded my deeper search for the divine.

Then, in yet a deeper introspective search of the previous romantic relationships I had been in, I recognized that in each of them there had been, in my perception, at least one component missing. I realized that although my relationships had been with nice men, there had been something I wanted from them that they were either unwilling or unable to give. One guy had a great sense of humor, but no money, and I wanted a man with, or well on his way to having, financial security. Another relationship was with a wealthy man, but he was critical and emotionally unavailable, and I wanted a man who could share his feelings. With yet another, there was a blazing fire, but he did not like my children.

For the first time ever, I realized that, since I am always in a relationship with my own hidden beliefs, I must have been carrying a hidden core belief that I can have *almost everything* with one man. This was a big aha moment for me! In light of exposing that hidden belief, which I recognized to be counter-intuitive to my desire and worthiness to have it *all*, I decided to change it. And so I did.

To be clear, I would like to mention that I do not believe that any one person can meet 100 percent of our needs completely, nor do I think they should be expected to do so. I am not a half looking for another half; rather I am a whole wanting to share that whole with another who wishes to share their whole being with me. The whole being is the culmination of what we evaluate as both the light and shadowed parts of the individual.

I do believe, however, that we can have a relationship with someone who is *naturally* congruent with our core desires and values. With this person, we will not feel deprived of anything. It was to this aim that I persevered in my quest for a relationship based on fullness, not lack.

I also believe that we can have both our core desire and our changing desires met within the parameters of a soulful relationship—it just takes some work and commitment to growing and evolving. Since my desire had shifted from being in a passionate pursuit of the divine to becoming passionate with Allan, we needed to talk, and so we did. Of course, it is reasonable to mention that the pursuit of the divine was inevitably moving me towards Allan, since there was no separation between them. This fact still at times escapes me, but I am *remembering* more often than I have in the past!

Transparency and Tears

In all honesty, the discussion we had on the topic of my pursuit of wanting fire in our relationship was a bit paralyzing; I had lain awake for hours before our morning discussion, wondering if I was only going to hurt, not heal, our relationship with my admission that the fire was gone. The discussion itself was both terrifying and liberating, and one of the hardest topics I had ever had to discuss with Allan. I needed to come right out and tell him that I had not felt fire for him since the period immediately following our short separation early in our relationship.

As a spiritual teacher and therapist, I knew that what would destroy our marriage the fastest were the things we thought about but wouldn't share. I decided that I couldn't hide my new yearning for fire, which had emerged in the preceding months, and concluded that if anyone needed to know how I was feeling, it was Allan. I recognized that if I couldn't tell him my truth, then the work of years of building an open-hearted, honest, and communicative relationship with Allan was an illusion. I believed that we had built our relationship on innocence, freedom, and trust, so this was our test to see if these qualities were still supporting our marriage.

I confessed to Allan that it had been months earlier, in June to be exact, when my yearning had begun to shift from God to man. Coincidentally, it was just as Venus was moving in the heavens to a new astrological position. With this, I experienced a long previously surrendered desire for deep sexual intimacy, more flirtation, and playful passion. Somewhere in this magical month was born within me the desire for fire in our marriage. For Allan, the message was bittersweet, because for years my interest and participation in our sexual intimacy had been less than he knew I was capable of. He welcomed my yearning for fire, yet my confession of not knowing whether I could feel it again with him was heartbreaking. We both felt bewildered, and I cried.

Since the union with Allan was built upon friendship, trust, kindness, parenthood, and Allan's adoration of me, it was also the first relationship in which the need for fire had been placed so low on my values list.

Fire had not been valued by me for so long—nine years—that I had forgotten its sweetness. I was reminded of it one day, when, quite unintentionally, I began talking, and then flirting, with a group of men in our business centre. I flirted, not because I was attracted to them, but because I suddenly remembered how good it felt to be playful with the opposite sex. My libido had suddenly come home!

Once the libido returned, I began to wonder why I had ever let my flirtatious nature slip away. Then I realized that in Allan's having a very high moral code, and in my valuing him so dearly in my life, I had unconsciously tucked away this part of my nature. I was a natural flirt when we met, but I suppose that I decided not to do anything that I thought might jeopardize our union. He had never shown a stitch of jealousy, so the suppressing of this part of my nature was my ego's doing alone.

Through some honest searching of my life and knowing that in truth, *there is never anything missing,* since energy is not created or destroyed but rather can only be transformed, I acknowledged that I had not really gone without fire all those years; it was just not in our sexual relationship. Instead, it was in my pursuit of the divine. It was also in my work as a therapist, mediator, author, and speaker, and most obviously in my passion for revealing the innocence and brilliance in people.

Since energy can be transformed, I needed to decide from where I was willing to take the fire so that it could be allocated predominance in our sexual relationship. I decided that the fire would come from all of the places where it had been. This meant that perhaps those areas would not be quite as fiery as they had been, but I was comfortable with that. In fact, perhaps it was time to play more and work less. To my surprise, this move or relocation of fire did not lessen my productivity; instead, it made me wiser in choosing what was worth pursuing and working on and with whom.

I discovered that the primary reason fire, passion, and chemistry between us had been extinguished was a feeling of being controlled. Fire is extinguished when we perceive ourselves to be controlled or in jeopardy of losing our perceived power.

We feel fire towards people whom we believe we can control and can equally be controlled by. It seems that fire is "fair exchange electricity." The arenas in which each soul will perceive they can control the other will vary. Remember, it is all a perceptual thing—the beloved, in our perception, will be a perfect blending of our parents' greatness, mixed with our unconscious yearning for the approval and appreciation of the parent whom we perceive to have been most disapproving of us.

People who perceive themselves as equals can elicit fire. Thus, with feelings of loss of control and power comes the loss of passion. Fire is often a sign of authentic power at play.

To reclaim my fire, I needed to become completely honest with myself in owning the truth that the way I had previously controlled men was through my passion, body, and sexuality. Because this was true, I realized that it must be what I perceived to be my greatest offering or treasure in a relationship. In short, it was my ace. So, Allan wanted my ace, and I, naturally, wanted his.

From my ego's perspective and evaluation, my husband did have something that I wanted. This something also needed to produce freedom and power like my ace did for him. His ace was his money. Through it, he had won me; it was his most prized possession. What I had that he wanted as badly as his money was my fire; what he had that I wanted and valued equally as my fire was his money. The forbidden "fruit" was exposed, and we each needed to bite. Later we realized that there had been an unspoken pact made silently between our egos that each of us could hold our respective ace, hopefully indefinitely. In so doing, we could forever usurp love's deepest passion — fire.

For years, my ego had quietly instructed, albeit unconsciously, that I was giving my husband just enough attention to keep him around and in the game, without needing to play, or rather offer up, my ace!

Let's consider the following: Both passion/fire and money/freedom have the ability to control others through power. Both can make one feel powerful, and both are coveted in our society. Also note that the violation or removal of either can also leave us feeling helpless, vulnerable, or raped. In this sense, for Allan and me, even what we were withholding was a mirror reflection of the other's "power tool."

As a part of the healing and uncovering of our hidden treasures, my husband acknowledged that he had always secretly wondered if some day I would "take" him financially. Energetically I knew that, and decided I would withhold my fire until he changed his mind. To clarify, the bargain struck between my soul and his was that if he surrendered his treasure, I would surrender mine.

My discovery of the underlying power struggle between us was felt as a truth deeply within us both. As Allan agreed to surrender his control of me through money, the spark was fanned into a raging fire!

What one can deduce from our experience is that fire, chemistry, and passion are the by-products of authentic freedom and safety. True passion emerges from a willingness to stand naked in front of each other without feeling controlled, imprisoned, or judged. Fire happens when "fair exchange" of our authentic self is present—when neither soul is holding out anything that is perceived dearer than each other's real self. Thus, true soulful chemistry is the melting in of our protective boundaries, which can occur only if we recognize there is nothing to protect against.

The Dynamics of Sexual Violation Energy

An exploration of "chemistry" would not be complete without a discussion of sexual violation energy—another kind of highly charged energy, which propagates unexplainable sexual attention and desire in people without their understanding. Sexual energy of this sort can fill the energy field of a person who has a memory of being sexually violated. This energy is "pointed" in that when it surrounds the field of a person who perceives that they have been a victim of sexual violation (real or imagined), bystanders will notice that they are drawn to focus on the sexual parts of the "victim." These individuals will unconsciously use their sexuality as a "power tool."

The sexual "attracted-ness" that surrounds the victim serves to lure in potential individuals (prey), so that the violated soul (or "victim") can regain control and manipulate, albeit unconsciously, through using their sexuality, in hopes of eventually healing their wound. When a person has been violated, they've experienced having their individual *will* seized. On a very deep unconscious level, the "victim" will want to have power over another in the same way that they had been overpowered.

This is an ego-driven attempt at healing that will give the "victim" a false sense of correction. Since the ego thinks that the only way to get rid of something you don't want (guilt, anger, shame, fear, or power-lessness) is through the "recreation" of an event, the same feelings of being overpowered energetically will be experienced by the "victim's victim." This time, the highly charged sexual energy that will move between the pair will feel addictive and overpowering.

In fact, individuals who perceive themselves to be victims of an uninvited sexual encounter carry sexual violation energy in their energetic field in order to seduce others with the hope of regaining whatever choice and freedom they perceive were taken. These individuals tend to be very charismatic and inviting in nature. Further, they unconsciously attract sexual partners with this seductive energy in order to get rid of their pain. However persistent the victim is in this methodology to heal the wound, it does not work, because they are emotionally unavailable to their suitors. For them, true emotional connective healing cannot occur until they undergo therapy geared towards revisiting their violation truthfully.

The therapy that truly heals individuals who have experienced sexual violation aims at revealing their core beliefs, even when these are based on self-depreciation and self-hate. The beliefs that would attract such an experience include, once again, the incessant desire for specialness. In particular, my findings have shown that individuals who suffer from low self-esteem and a depreciated self-worth are most at risk for attracting a sexual violation experience.

In my work with individuals who have experienced sexual violation, I have found that when such a person searches deeply and honestly, they often discover that they desperately wished to feel special and wanted—sometimes so much that they get both desires met through unconsciously inviting the assault. Also, they discover that the encounter between them and their perpetrator was indeed preceded by an intuitive warning that they overrode instead of heeded. Further, they realize that as a result of the experience, they never again dismissed that kind of warning in any area of their life. Lastly, most sexually violated individuals discover, as I did through an incident of sexual violation that I experienced in my youth, that overcoming the hurt resulting from the violation is an important aspect of the soul work they have come to earth to do.

Women and men who carry intense feelings of abandonment or rejection by a parent, for example girls with their fathers and boys with their mothers, will sometimes unconsciously attract such a violation to help them work through their feelings. June, a client of mine, who once lived an extremely provocative lifestyle and would turn "tricks" when cash or drugs were needed, has agreed to let me share her story:

> *I adored my dad, but he was never around. He was always away on business. I felt invisible. I had a huge desire to be noticed by my dad. Years passed, and eventually I turned towards flirting with boys to get the much-wanted male attention. I flirted and teased, to feel seen, valued, and "special." Then, one day, I was gang-raped. I told no one at first because I felt partially responsible. Then, about a year later, I began to seduce and control guys sexually. When my parents finally found out that I had been raped, I felt powerful. Dad finally "saw" me.*
>
> *My healing from the incident only came once I admitted that I wanted to feel powerful just like the gang did. I wanted to control others as much as I had felt powerless, and I used sex to get what I wanted, just as did the boys in the gang.*

It is truly amazing to uncover how our core beliefs attract both the people and the circumstances that will force us to stand up for ourselves and empower us to make choices based on love instead of fear. If, on the other hand, we are not yet able to make choices based upon self-love, our sexual violation experience will become an excuse for us to use our bodies through acts of promiscuity, and our emotions in ways that are meant to entrap rather than free our "dance partners." We do so in our search for power, and to feel in control, since control and choice appear to have been taken from us when we were violated. The shameless truth is, if we feel violated, we will violate in some form or fashion, in order to heal ourselves and those we attract. This is because the CAB Principle© will become operative, which states that we will *create, attract,* or *become* anything we do not love.

We cannot assume, however, that all individuals who act promiscuously have been violated. Some people, in particular teenage girls, many of whom have been hypnotized through advertising campaigns and idols such as Britney Spears, sometimes connect sexuality with power and desirability, and so they use their bodies as instruments to secure both. Sadly in our society today, we have bought into the idea that sex is power, and our marketing campaigns prove that sex sells.

It is important for us to understand that we have access to power in different forms. It is critical to note that there is no power like authentic power, which is the power of a loving mind. When we fail to recognize this, we may be easily persuaded to use the body inappropriately in order to achieve what we desire.

How does unhealed sexual violation energy impact a committed relationship? When we have been sexually intruded upon, we hold a distorted view of the proper use of our genitals, sexuality, power, and control. As "victims" we become prone to using our sexuality as bait, or we use it to reward. While it is true that even those who have not been sexually violated use such methods to control their partner in a relationship, the energy that surrounds sexually violated individuals who display this behavior is different. The energy of the sexually violated person is addictive, electric, and seductive in nature, while the energy of someone who is trying to gain control or favor with their partner will feel more manipulative than addictive to the recipient.

Lastly, individuals who carry sexual violation energy tend to dress more provocatively to attract new "prey," so that they can again begin the cycle of attracting what they have not loved.

One advantage of marriage is that,
when you fall out of love with him
or
he falls out of love with you,
it keeps you together
until you fall in again.

Judith Viorst

Chapter Five

Why We Marry "Our Parents"

It was 1998 when I discovered, quite unexpectedly, that I had married the embodiment of my mother's most predominant traits—the traits I most associated with pain and rejection. I needed to learn how to love those traits, so that I could learn how to love myself fully and, consequently, more deeply. This was accomplished through the transformative dance called marriage on three different occasions, with three different men, over a 25-year period!

What I want to illuminate is that the men I chose to marry had the same domineering qualities that my mother had. The traits were the ones from which I had disassociated myself, but which were indeed within my nature, unnoticed by me. Although at first I did not recognize this to be true, in time I discovered that I used these same traits in order to gain power, just like my mother and husbands had done, although I was passively aggressive, rather than overtly like my mother.

The traits I most disliked were associated with attributes incorporating controlling, domineering, manipulation, intimidation, and emotionally distanced behaviors. My fear and dislike of these traits had developed because in my childhood, *I had connected them with feelings of helplessness and powerlessness.* For me, then, those particularly uncomfortable traits and my unsettling emotional responses became inseparable "bedfellows." Further, since I did not know how to appreciate them, I avoided them and failed to mature into authentic adulthood emotionally.

It would be accurate to say that behaviors that my parents had acted out, particularly my mom, and that had left me feeling powerless, controlled, vulnerable, or insecure, stunted or stalled my emotional maturing. In a very real sense, then, I was both a mature and responsible woman and a frightened, emotionally immature child. Over the span of 25 years, each husband would encounter different ages of my emotional child—an emotional self that would, over time, move from toddlerhood through adolescence, and then into early and finally fully matured adulthood. So, it is fair to say that our marital unions encourage our growing up, much like our parents were fundamental to our maturing into socially functioning adults.

My perception of traits that fostered the feeling of being overwhelmed led me to believe that I had no control, and that I had limited choices whenever anyone displayed these traits. I therefore avoided those individuals at all cost. Since the foundational principle of love is that we learn how to love and appreciate all things we have not yet appreciated, the previously mentioned CAB Principle© kicked in, according to which we will *create, attract,* or *become* anything we do not love. Because I had not loved these traits in my mother, my soul directed me to another opportunity that would allow me to do so through marriage.

For most of us, when we experience someone being dishonest or manipulative, we feel disempowered because we do not have all the information we believe we require. The fact that an individual has chosen to be this way with us is reflective of our own level of disempowerment, which in turn they are bringing to us through the experience so that we can learn to love that facet of our nature. Because in my evaluation, being in a dance with these traits meant that I had lost power, this became my experience. It was not really true—it was only true for me because my beliefs governed my experiences. However, since I had not been shown that my perception was an evaluation based upon what I had observed as a child, I was destined to live it out until I grew beyond the belief. In watching my parents' responses to each other when either of them deployed these traits, I knew no other connection between these "bedfellows" until one day I chose a different response to those traits than the one I had witnessed. I chose instead to observe and own the truth that I, too, used those traits when I felt powerlessness. Until that new choice emerged—one of compassion and ownership—I believed that powerlessness was the only outcome that could come from anyone dancing with those traits. Suddenly, I realized that I had come to the earth, and had chosen my parents and husbands, to heal this association. Innocently, I had connected the two, and innocently I could choose to disconnect them, too.

Owning the Disowned

Since all of my evaluations of the traits—controlling, domineering, intimidation, manipulation, and emotional distancing—shaped my belief in my own self-worth, I was contracted to not only attract these traits from within men's natures, but I also needed to learn how to love and appreciate them in myself. As I became able to do so, my self-love and self-worth expanded. Eventually, I realized that I had married these "motherly traits" in order to recognize that none of them had power over my authentic identity, nor did I need to avoid them any longer.

The recognition that we marry partners who portray aspects of our parents fascinated me, and so I became increasingly interested in discovering all the parts of my parents with which I was interacting as an adult. Through my adulthood, I was able to heal my childhood perceptions and mature in selfhood.

I explored further to see the ways in which I had become romantically involved with the emotional, physical, psychological, mental, and spiritual beliefs, attributes, and traits of my parents. Interestingly, I realized that I was sexually most attracted to men who demonstrated the traits and qualities of my father that I had most associated with love, comfort, security, and safety—men with whom I felt I could be safe in expressing the vulnerable feminine side of my nature. There was an ache to be in a surrendered yet safe place, and it worked like a powerful magnetic field. It deeply affected both my psyche and my body chemistry, which sparked *fire*! These men were also those who would inevitably leave me, just like my dad had done when I was seven. Again, I realized that the CAB Principle© was in effect, and would remain so, until such a time that I could appreciate his leaving my life.

This strange mix of marrying "mom," yet being smitten by "dad," helped me to realize that my fantasy man was a mixture of both. As I mentioned in the section *The Chemistry of Passionate Love* in chapter four, the mate of my dreams possessed all the traits I loved in my parents, with the dominating physical attributes of my dad. My presumption is that in my early childhood, I had identified with the idea that dad offered safety and protection. It seems that he also reflected my idea of what God must be like, which is how most young children see their parents.

Because I had associated with my feelings of powerlessness and worth, my mother was the one for whom I felt I could never be good enough. The therapy came in the form of "marrying" her, three times over, in hopes of finally being good enough.

My mother was a gypsy—an entrepreneur and an intelligent, charismatic individual who could mesmerize both men and women. She had an insatiable hunger to understand and know God. She was both generous and a humanitarian, and she believed that the rich should give to the poor—let's just say she was an embodiment of Robin Hood!

The Dynamics of Projection

Mom was also a soul who, in my perception, placed the bar of achievement very high. Whenever I felt unable to reach it, I associated her response (emotional distancing, intimidation, manipulation) with rejection. It is important to note that her facial expressions, and what I saw to be emotional distancing, were probably unrelated to the situation for which I was seeking acknowledgment. In fact, she was most likely unaware of the fact that I was linking the two, since projection is largely based upon the past, not the present situation.

It should also be noted that I did reach the bar often, but not always. Interestingly, however, my ego's voice never pointed out my acknowledgments and achievements—instead it liked to point out the failures. Since my ego said I had failed, I assumed that my mother thought the same.

The following were the overriding beliefs that I *chose* to extract from my "dance" with my mother:

- I am as good as the degree to which my achievements are valued.
- I am able to do anything I set my mind to.
- I can manipulate men with my sexuality.
- It is more spiritual to be a martyr.
- You will love me more if I prove that I can do it by myself.
- You will want me more if I remain emotionally distant.
- I should sacrifice my wants to be with you— that is what love does.
- To protect my heart from you is both necessary and wise.
- Fidelity does not establish the presence of love.

My father, who left my life when I was seven, was handsome, hardworking, and a protector. He liked guns, and he was an absolute people pleaser. He was warm-hearted, very committed, and worked as a purser on commercial aircrafts. He was not around much. I loved to see him in his uniform, with his hat (which looked like a pilot's cap) and perfectly polished black patent shoes. He was my idol, and everything I hoped to marry someday! From him I extracted the following beliefs;

- Blond-haired, rounded-faced men will reject and abandon me.
- They have power and passion, and must be controlled.
- They are committed to their goals and needs, not mine.
- If you do not show them they are loved, they will leave, no matter what.
- To stay safe, you must play with them—not commit to them.
- Surrender and defenselessness will mean loss and heartbreak, so it should be avoided at all cost.
- Blond men are charismatic and funny.

Please note the striking differences between the fragmented beliefs that I extracted from each of my parents. From my mother, I developed a strong sense of identity—a sense of self. From my father, I created ideas about men in general. Both my parents contributed to my learning of what traits and physical attributes I associated with love and fear.

So, why would anyone marry the embodiment of one of their parents when they grow up? The primary reason is that our parents' traits show us what we do or did not love about ourselves. Through marrying "our parents," we are able to reconstruct the marriage we witnessed our parents to be in, in hopes of doing it "right." We unconsciously want to relive and repair anything we perceive they did that caused them or us pain, and to set it right. Through marrying our parents' counterparts, we have an opportunity to learn that we are, and always have been, good enough.

As children, we fashion our core beliefs of worthiness around the degree to which we perceive that our parents approve of us. However, since our beliefs are based upon our perceptions and evaluations as children, our beliefs of worthiness are often immature and limited in awareness and understanding.

For us as adults, it is imperative to the success of our marriages and the raising of our children that we come to love and appreciate all of our parents' traits—in other words, "heal with our parents." In short, we need to love any previously unloved memories or traits that we share with them.

When we were children, we watched and "digested" our parents' relationship and then grew up to "repattern" them, in order to learn to love and appreciate that which we had not loved about their relationship dynamic as children. In our childhood, we watched our parents control each other and assessed what they did, so that we could learn what did and didn't work in their attempts to attain power or control. We made countless associations between what they said and did, and established ideas of the way a relationship should be. Consequently, we later unconsciously recreated their relationship, in hopes of correcting their errors and doing things differently than what was modeled to us.

The CAB Principle©

However committed we were to not recreating the relationship that our parents had, the pervading CAB Principle surfaced again to ensure that we would *create, attract,* or *become* that which we had not loved.

Because the CAB Principle is a key transformative mechanism within the new marriage paradigm, we come to realize that there are more than just two sets of dynamics surrounding the parties in a soulful relationship. There are the beliefs of the adults within the relationship and the unconscious and wounded associations that were formed in childhood "playing out."

By way of an example, let's look at how these dynamics would play out in my relationship with Allan:

1. Allan being influenced by his relationship with his father, which he projects onto his relationship with me.
2. Allan being influenced by his relationship with his mother, which he projects onto his relationship with me.
3. I being influenced by my relationship with my father, which I project onto my relationship with Allan.
4. I being influenced by my relationship with my mother, which I project onto my relationship with Allan.
5. Allan's current relationship with me.
6. My current relationship with Allan.
7. Allan's healed and integrated life-learning relationship dynamics (including all of his

previous romantic encounters) in relation to me.

8. My healed and integrated life-learning relationship dynamics (including all my previous romantic encounters) in relation to Allan.

In the soulful relationship, the couple is aware and appreciative of the two (and, as we have just explored, up to eight) separate relationships, all integrating emotions ranging from fear to love through their "dance." To illustrate using the example of my relationship, there is a set of dynamics between Allan and me as adults, and there is Allan's idea of his relationship with me as it is triggered by beliefs formed by his relationship with his father. Then, there are dynamics formed between him and me that are influenced by beliefs he formed from interactions with his mother. On my end, of course, there are also the dynamics formed from my childhood relations with my parents. All these relationships are then tumbled together to create a fascinating and fertile ground to heal and integrate the souls.

This integrative work is accomplished by helping each soul learn what is true about them and what is a protective covering that must eventually be shed. With certainty, each individual will come to recognize how to love and appreciate their authentic selves which were once hidden beneath illusions.

A model for these dynamics is post-secondary education, where we choose a "major" and sometimes also a "minor" field towards gaining mastery in our chosen profession. This same model applies to the education we achieve through marriage and romantic relationships. Each individual will have chosen a parent as a major and one as a minor subject. In my case, my mother was and is my "major" area of healing and self-esteem growth. So, symbolically, I am married to my mom, but do see more and more of my father's qualities emerging in my husband over time.

Allan, in marrying me, chose a spouse who mirrors the characteristics of his dad, although there are minor qualities of his mom embodied in my nature. The "eight of us" make for interesting bedfellows, to say the least. The power in understanding the dynamic in which so many personalities interact helps me to sift through what is true and what is false because it is based upon past wounds. In knowing this, Allan and I are less likely to blame each other and are more likely to remain open-hearted as we recognize our parents' traits in each other and learn to love them.

In marriage, as each soul integrates the traits of their parents within their own soul nature, they also experience those same traits with their parental figures as being healed. As a result, there is more ease and there are more peace-filled moments for the couple to share. Because a key factor of relationship is learning to love and own our once disowned or shadowed parts, the couple's parents are also part of the couple's make-up and also of each identity within the relationship, and so the marriage truly becomes an island of refuge for future generations to rest upon.

The dominant traits that I most disliked in my mother, and which I also perceive and dislike in Allan, are being controlling, holding too high an expectation, emotional distancing, intimidation, always wanting to be right, holding grudges, and pouting. This identifies what I still dislike in myself. As I grow in appreciation of those traits in myself, they will appear to be minimized in him. The truth is that they will be loved in me, so I will not see them as dominant in him, either.

A great exercise for a couple wishing to transform their relationship from the old to the new paradigm is to list the top ten qualities that each likes and dislikes in their parents. Then each person should look for those same traits in themselves, although they may show up in different ways or areas in their life. Lastly, they should look for them in their mate. Next, they should identify as many positive aspects of the traits as possible. Each will grow in appreciation of these once disliked traits, and love is sure to follow!

The Fantasy of the Ideal Mate

The following is the story of a couple with whom I worked several years ago. It clearly illustrates the extent to which our parents, their relationship, our core belief system, and our perception of our upbringing, have influenced our relationships.

Helen had come to see me, hoping to understand her quickly descending feelings for her husband of only 18 months. I asked her what was going on at home and at work. At home, she said that Sam was farming and keeping the house in order. She said that she loved him, but also carried a lot of resentment about the fact that he was not helping her with her business. She said that she had agreed to marry him provided he would help her establish her longtime dream of owning an equestrian wellness center. In addition, she stated that they had agreed they would eventually buy a piece of land and move their modular home off the land owned by Sam's parents. Now, however, Sam wanted to stay on the parental homestead. He felt safe and secure, and believed it to be less financially stressful than purchasing a large piece of land on which to erect the wellness center. He and Helen had strongly opposing views on this issue.

Sam had been raised by down-to-earth people who believed in keeping things simple. His parents believed that family was everything and family members owed each other support. They were a "salt-of-the-earth" traditional couple. Sam's father raised livestock, and his mother was a homemaker and devoted caregiver.

Helen came from what she perceived to be an impoverished childhood environment. Her mom was a single parent who struggled for everything. "We had our basic needs met, but there were no designer jeans," Helen said. She was a driven, hardworking, and extremely talented animal caregiver and healer. She worked 60 to 70 hours a week, and was both exhausted and disheartened with the relationship. The couple had not been sexually intimate in over a year.

I soon discovered that Helen held within her mind an image of what an ideal husband would do. Sam, too, held an image of what an ideal wife would be. Neither of them reflected the ideal that their partner held, nor were they able to communicate these ideals and hopes to one another because anger and frustration had so contaminated the relationship.

Helen wanted Sam to do some light bookkeeping and billing for the services she rendered. Sam wanted Helen to help him understand details connected with the clients being billed. Helen perceived his questioning as a way to escape the work. Sam felt justified in bookmarking the work, not having been given the information he thought was needed to do it. They were at an impasse.

Sam felt like he was an unappreciated "slave" of Helen's, which made him angry. "Helen does not acknowledge that I work hard, too!" he said.

Helen, following a ten- to twelve-hour work day, would find Sam watching TV when she got home and felt that she was the only one working towards fulfilling the "dream."

Soon, Sam no longer really cared about the "dream," since he had begun to wonder if or when Helen would ever be satisfied. His greatest fear was that she would never feel satisfied with how the dream was expressed—whether there would ever be enough buildings, animals, etc. Feeling defeated, he chose to shut down. He felt that, although she was working incredibly long hours, she was not happy, nor would she ever be, since this "dream" was running her life, and their relationship.

Helen felt betrayed by Sam and disheartened. She had lost respect for him as a man and partner, and consequently the desire for sex evaporated. No healthy person wants to be sexually intimate with either their parent or child, so if either person begins to view their mate that way, intimacy will erode.

Helen had fallen into a classic intimacy-disabling role of becoming Sam's "mother," viewing him as a "child," which could not embrace, protect, and nourish her dream of the equestrian wellness center. Since her dream was in a sense her "baby," she felt as though both she and the "baby" had been abandoned. The result was a predictable power struggle that emerged between the pair, and which further crippled feelings of intimacy between them.

In awakening feelings of parent-child dynamics in the couple, each of them elicited within the other any unresolved wounds they respectively had with their own parents—Helen with her mom, and Sam with his mom. Since we all carry some "stuff" from our relationship with our parents, and we all felt at times overpowered by them, this dance in a marriage is largely unavoidable. These childhood feelings of disempowerment and inequality of power drive us into unconscious power struggles in our marriages.

When Helen stepped into the role of Sam's "mother," she unknowingly drew out unvisited issues that Sam had with his mom in respect of his wanting to feel like a capable strong man, and not her little boy. In a nutshell, Helen in this role was making him feel like a boy, not a man, so he in turn acted like a boy, which perpetuated the cycle. The more she mothered him, the more he became defiant, and unwilling to birth the "baby." The more he withdrew, the more she withheld sex.

At the time this couple came to see me, Helen valued her equestrian wellness center more than Sam, since her center was "missing," and Sam was not. Sam resented this, until I reminded him that, in her mind, he was not missing. Remember that voids drive our priorities and values! Both Sam and Helen wondered how and if they could ever reconcile their different natures, values, and goals.

Following a session with each of them, it was clear to me that they loved each other, but that, as a couple, they had lost sight of what had pulled them together. I warned Sam that if he did not truly want to pursue Helen's dream yet continued to follow it, he would burn out. He acknowledged that he already felt that way.

I suggested to Helen that, if Sam did not want to embrace her dream in his life and thus, in part, make it his own, their relationship was headed for completion. She, too, realized this. She struggled with the dialogue between her head and her heart. She wanted to have both Sam and her dream. Sam wanted her and her happiness, and to have some sexual intimacy.

Sam wanted to know if Helen would ever be satisfied that she had enough material comfort. I assured him that, although the drive was coming from her perceived lack in childhood and the desire to show her mom that she could "do it," I felt she would be satisfied when she achieved her dream. This brought him comfort, but I also advised him that Helen would need to make a commitment of that nature to him.

Sam realized that he had been so resentful of the "dream" that he was not doing things to help them move towards it. He understood that he was unconsciously detouring them as a way of punishing Helen for not being happy or wanting to be intimate with him. Following this recognition, he agreed to make some compromises and to redirect his work toward the dream. He was willing to sell the cattle and find a piece of land and prepare it for the relocation of their modular home. He also agreed to take more contract work and try to increase his annual income, provided the expectation of home-making and cooking would be waived.

Helen agreed to settle with a smaller piece of land to get a mini-version of the center operating. She agreed to give Sam the information needed to do the books. She agreed to continue counseling to get them talking more, which would eventually rebuild respect and the desire for sexual intimacy.

Both Sam and Helen needed to discover that they had been letting the wishes and fantasy of how their parents' lives unfolded govern and dominate their relationship. They each began to understand how they thought differently, and learned to use those differences as strengths. Once they had broken the fantasy expectation, they were back on track to a soulful, rather than a "special," relationship.

When we create an ideal of what a mate should be, it is driven by the belief that if we had that ideal mate, we would be happy. We fantasize that with the dream mate, we would no longer feel disappointed, and we wouldn't need to be reminded of the childhood memories that we find uncomfortable and painful. This fantasy mate is composed of all that we perceive as void within our lives and natures. In fact, it is the things we think are missing within ourselves, such as adoration, acceptance, value, and approval, that we desperately seek from another, but don't give to ourselves. Once we grow sufficiently in self-love, however, we then give these things to ourselves, and thus we free our mate from the "fantasy bondage" under which we had placed the relationship.

Success in marriage does not come merely through finding the right mate, but through being the right mate.

Barnett R. Brickner

Chapter Six

How Values Drive Relationships

For the most part, we have bought into the belief that whenever our relationship or marriage ends, it is due to a breakdown in communication or a failure on the part of the couple. I think such a belief is erroneous, deeply despairing, and disheartening, let alone completely untrue. In fact, to assume that we could attract and pair with, or marry, the "wrong" person is quite an egotistical idea.

Each person with whom we pair is ultimately the "right" person, because they will inevitably reflect our *current* thoughts and beliefs, and the traits we both admire and despise about ourselves in some mysterious way. Further, during the union, our mates have the necessary and perfect lesson of love that we are destined to learn in order to evolve. This is *why* they have come and remain in relationship with us. It is as if each intimate partner with whom we have danced, are currently dancing, or will dance, gives back to us a part of ourselves we felt was missing. When we have *learned what they have come to teach,* and claimed our authentic power, the relationship may complete *in that form.*

Ultimately, all relationships continue forever because of the unassailable growth that occurs for both souls. This whole process nurtures the awakening and awareness of our authentic selves as beings of love. It is important to note that we can never move backwards in our awareness of self. We cannot "unknow" that which we have learned, we can only forget that we know, and we all do this at times.

Our ability to create our deepest desires fluctuates in proportion to our awareness and acceptance of our authentic self. Consequently, we all have differing speeds at which we feel safe and comfortable in "awakening." Because of these preferences, we require different people who will "mirror" our rate of awakening, at different periods in our life. Everyone is expanding in some way and at some speed, and we are all increasing in our knowledge of self. The question is, which *self* are we feeding and expanding? The one we feed is the one that will grow. Depending upon which self it is—the authentic self or the ego—we will be attracting a particular mate to help us achieve our goal. It is important to note that we all fluctuate between feeding both the real and imagined self throughout our lifetime. We do, however, eventually decide to focus primarily on the authentic self, once we have discovered that the acquisitions of this world cannot satisfy our soul.

The truth is, all of us are *already* purely as we were created to be—a being that *is* love and abundance—and we are, therefore, really not in need of anything. And it *is* the goal of every soulful relationship to bring us closer to that realization. Remember that all special relationships are built upon the belief that we are guilty, unlovable, and lacking in character and in the attainment of material assets of some kind. The goal of the soulful relationship, however, is to encounter and heal anything real or imagined that closes the heart. Further, the goal of soulful love relationships is to share one's innate fullness, innocence, and abundance, rather than search for it externally.

Love Knows No Judgment

From the perspective of the awakened soul, the completion of a relationship occurs when the goal of the souls has been met in the relationship. And the ultimate goal of every human is to grow and learn to love themselves fully. This is accomplished in part through loving our partner as they are without judgment, coupled with the relationship dynamics that will help us grow in our understanding and appreciation of our deeper nature—our authentic self. Because we do not always have conscious awareness of how that goal is achieved, we are generally too quick to decide that the relationship must have failed because it does not meet our fantasy expectations of what soul growth encompasses.

The ego's objective is to destroy the relationship through the avoidance of love, disempowerment, the enforcement of judgment, and the addiction to guilt placed upon whomever the ego deems appropriate, so that it can "feel better." If this objective is overturned by love, then the ego will try to convince us that the relationship breakup is indicative of our failures. Because the objectives of the ego within the relationship are all based upon guilt, fear, autonomy, exclusion, and revenge, the idea of marriage completion as a success is unimaginable to the ego, which considers marriage completion as one more score in its attacks against you.

Since we have discovered that we *only* attract ourselves to us and that the way our mate treats us is a direct reflection of the ways we treat ourselves, *no mistake* can be made by any partner. Quite to the contrary, then, we will understand that relationships *complete naturally* when one or both souls have loved and integrated all that they had joined together to do. And since we are unaware of the larger soul contract between any two souls, or the family dynamics that all have agreed to heal, we are ill informed when advising each other that our marriage is breaking down, based upon our limited understanding of what, from the soul's perspective, was an authentic soul advancement towards increased self-love of either the micro-self (the individual soul) or the macro-self—the collective of all those who participate in the marriage dance. The macro-self includes the dynamics revolving around the traits of our parents that we are still learning to love.

Another common mistake I often come across is the belief that, if we do all the relationship things "right," we will be guaranteed a lifelong partnership. This, too, is an illusion. Love does not possess, nor does it seek to exclude anyone from anyone else, so the desire for a lifelong pairing is itself an indicator that the relationship is moving from soulful back into special relationship dynamics.

I do not subscribe to the breakdown belief, and I work with couples who are either preparing to lovingly travel down their differing soulful paths, or with couples who have decided to transform their marriage into the new paradigm.

Relationships between people are eternal, regardless of their physical proximity, or the differing categories we place around them such as friend, ex-wife, girlfriend, or neighbor. They are eternal because souls do leave fingerprints upon one another's hearts from being touched in ways that teach us that our authentic self is lovable beyond measure, and that we have encountered one another to find and uphold that self. The painful polishing away of all the beliefs that once informed us that we were bound, im-poverished, lacking, unlovable, or at the effect of fear in any way is what makes every encounter a holy one. This is the objective of the voice of truth within us. It is for this reason that we define the completion of a relationship as a success, rather than a breakdown.

The voice of truth acts as a memory of our authentic self, just as the ego is a wish and memory of an inauthentic self. The primary goals of the voice of truth and the ego are diametrically opposed to one another. As we identify ourselves with either the voice of truth or the ego, truth-based or fear-based thoughts will be issued in the mind. We must make the decision on whether we want the voice of truth or the ego to orchestrate our relationship.

It is usually in the eleventh hour of our pain that we are most willing to look at our relationship and ourselves to find the truth. Gratefully, inherent within us is the ancient knowing that the truth will set us free, and so we turn to prayer and ask for help. The help comes through the voice of truth, which is within our minds.

Through my work with couples, I have discovered that even when things seem to be very difficult, there is still the opportunity for tremendous growth for the couple and for fostering self-awareness, and therefore love.

Identifying Couple Values

To facilitate the process of deciding whether a couple should stay together or prepare to complete the marriage dance, we discuss the differing and similar values, beliefs, expectations, and desires that each individual has.

I assist the couple in their understanding that going through difficult times in their relationship is a blessing because it propagates a deeper questioning for each to decide what they want from their relationship. In addition, I help the couple to recognize that their life and relationship do, in fact, reflect where their true values are. Further, difficult times indicate that their values and desires are changing as a result of increased self-love on the part of one or both partners. Therefore, the desire to address the unhappiness within the marriage should be celebrated, since it illuminates the importance that the relationship has had, and will have, on their overall state of well-being.

When a couple is unhappy with the interactions and level of intimacy between them, yet does nothing to change them, it is because their relationship has not been one of their top values, or because one or both of them are afraid of becoming more transparent and intimate. As I probe further into the situation by asking deeper questions, they usually discover that their kids, financial security, stability, social pressure, or careers have been of greater importance. This happens in part because the proposition to get emotionally closer to each other is a desire the ego avoids, because love dissolves the ego. In short, emotional intimacy dissolves all our protective boundaries, and our sense of self must change. The ego despises change, and consequently quickly redirects the mate to secure themselves externally with more "stuff" in the form of money, cars, power, and so on. Since the acquisition of security through attainment of material wealth is one of the primary objectives of the ego, the deepening of love is "shelved" until one of the partners recognizes their deeper, insatiable hunger for love and refuses to settle for anything less.

I try to raise the couple's awareness of the fact that these other priorities often take precedence until one or both of them decide that they want and deserve more—and that wanting more is a sign of emotional maturing. In fact, through increased self-love, they realize that they deserve to have it all, so they want love and fulfillment in all the other areas of their life that are important to them.

The decision to pursue and have success in all areas of life is indicative of increased self-love, self-worth, and self-appreciation on the part of the evolving soul, or souls. So, when I have the privilege of working with an individual whose consciousness is expanding, I am certain of their success. My certainty is derived from knowing that when we are aligning with our authentic nature, the natural result is a more love-filled life. The truth is that we all deserve deeply enriched lives congruent with our true identity as the abundant children of love.

Alternatively, when we feel that we do not have the skills to transform our relationship from the dynamics of "special" to "soulful"—meaning from autonomous to unified; from lack to fullness; from guilt to innocence; and from protectiveness to defenselessness—we usually want to run and hide from the relationship altogether because of the way "specialness" makes us feel about ourselves.

If, on the contrary, we can find the courage to identify the core ideals, values, beliefs, and desires that each soul hopes for in the marriage relationship, and if the couple can feel worthy of having those aspirations met *now*, they will have begun the journey towards determining whether or not they are both traveling in the same direction. If an open-hearted evaluation reveals to the couple that they are indeed being drawn towards differing life paths, each soul will be supported in proceeding in the direction of their soul's yearning without guilt or the belief that failure or a breakdown are the reason for the diverging paths.

To determine what our continuously changing core values and beliefs are, we can make adjustments to keep the relationship empowering for each mate. Because our values fluctuate and change as we perceive things such as money, health, fitness, and our careers to be missing, we need to check in with each other to illuminate those changes. Since we have a vision of what *for us* is a satisfactory level of order and organization as it pertains to a particular value we are holding, we do need to check in with our mate on an ongoing basis. In addition, we may even discover that there is a new assignment of priorities in an area of our mate's life that we are not all that interested in. Sharing and listening for changing values and priorities in our partner are essential for relationship growth, stability, and continued feelings of being cared for.

For instance, one of my current top values is the writing of this book, which means that, in my mind, the book is in part "missing," since it is not completed. Allan is aware of this currently missing goal because I opt out of other activities we normally do together, in order to write. Once the book is finished, writing will fall lower on my values list, and the riding of our motorcycles will probably rise up, since it has been "missing" while I chose to write instead of ride. However, when once again I become inspired to write another book, writing will again hit the top ten of my fluctuating values, as motorbike riding, or any other perceived lower-priority activity, will decrease.

One of Allan's current top values is the renovation of our home. When he has completed the upgrades in every room, renovating will fall dramatically down on his list. If I am wise, I will try to write *while* he is renovating. In doing so, we will both be better able to appreciate the other's values, since each brings the opportunity to do what we individually want to do. This will trigger a perception within our minds that states, "You can pursue what you love and participate in it without a 'cost' to me, as I can participate in my priorities without a 'price' to you." Connecting each of our differing values to support our individual pursuits eliminates the idea of sacrifice in love, which is what we aim to do in the soulful relationship. For instance, I am so committed to the connection of our values that I began writing as soon as I saw Allan pull out his tools to upgrade some home fixtures.

As I am writing this section of the book, Allan is replacing electrical plate covers in our home. Therefore, the ongoing work of connecting our shifting values is another important step towards upholding caring interactions between us. Knowing and appreciating each other's priorities and values are among the most important maintenance tools in our marriage.

Another powerful tool that facilitates the soulful relationship is gratitude. In particular, I have found that as I count my blessings as they relate to having Allan as a mate, I have been able to give more of my emotional self to him.

When we feel grateful, we also feel abundant. When we feel abundant, we are generous and are therefore more willing to give in ways and in areas where, at other times, we may be unwilling to give. Authentic emotional and psychological giving cannot occur when we're feeling emotionally impoverished. When we give from the "bankrupt" state, we usually take on the role of martyr, instead of being a caring and nurturing mate. In addition, our partner will feel indebted, rather than appreciative, as they will undoubtedly be required to pay us back for the "giving." The "price tag" of guilt will then have been attached to the sacrifice connected with the giving. This vicious cycle defines entrapment. The freedom and gratitude one usually feels for a partner who has shared themselves from a state of fullness and abundance are then assailed by the guilt.

Consequently, true giving can only come from a state of abundance, and gratitude is its natural result.

For me, then, counting my blessings is imperative to the success of my relationship with Allan, particularly in the area of participation in sexual intimacy. Allan's desire for sexual intimacy and my playful involvement in it are directly related to the level of gratefulness I am feeling at the time we are being intimate. My gratitude and appreciation rise, as does my libido, through contemplating the many blessings I have as a result of being with him and having him as my soul partner. Making and keeping a mental gratitude list of the benefits of my relationship with him keeps us close. This is particularly significant when I am focused on what I deem to be temporarily more important than sex. Gratitude, which nurtures generosity, is one of the secrets of a caring and loving soul-filled relationship, and becomes a foundational brick in the new marriage paradigm.

In the old paradigm of marriage, we believed that we needed to walk and live on a single path. We believed that the two people in the relationship needed to be woven together to succeed, and that sacrifice was a part of the marriage dance. Conversely, in the new marriage paradigm, we are supported in walking on paralleling paths, which may or may not continue in the same direction at all times. We are not asked to sacrifice, but rather to compromise our fixations on the beliefs that our expectations are the only things that matter. We instead grow in appreciation of our mate, and thus of ourselves, through the connecting of our differing goals and aspirations. In doing so, we come to the awareness that no matter what either mate does, it is for the benefit and the soul growth of the pair. In soulful relationships, we further acknowledge that we have been brought together so that we might learn how to love anything we have resisted loving because of a lack of understanding and knowledge.

Through my work as a marriage coach, I have witnessed that when one or both parties refuse to surrender their belief of how the relationship, or the other person, ought to be, the conclusion of their dance is fast approaching. Further, it is when we do not take the time or care to discover and support the achievement of our partner's values and priorities that the relationship begins to deteriorate. When one of the souls is under the belief that they are more important than their mate, they manifest the seesaw relationship.

In this model, the ego on the high seat is enacting carelessness toward the mate. In short, the ego is saying, "I do not care what you think, feel, or want. In fact, I have such deeply hidden feelings of power-lessness (of which I am unaware) that I must control you in order to feel good and worthy enough to function in the world. Your job is to allow me to continue this careless behavior so that I can feel good enough in at least one area of my life. I am never going to admit this, however."

On the opposite side of the seesaw is the careful soul. This ego in the low seat is saying, "I do not really matter. I feel grateful that someone of your stature, beauty, or intelligence could actually want to be with me. My worth is eroded over time, and I have the perception that I have never been good enough. I consequently feel worthless inside. I do not believe that I deserve to be treated with respect, since I associate respect with power. I have adopted the role of being a martyr, since it is a passive way to gain strength, and I can at least use guilt to maneuver in the relationship, and control you. I feel a huge sense of rage inside, which I conceal in passive-aggressive behavior, because I believe that you have all the control. In time, I will get so upset that I will begin to make changes in order to unbar myself from your controlling prison. When I do so, you will see a part of my nature that you have been expressing for years, but that I have been repressing. Your job is to eventually push the bar of expectations so high that I will finally take control and stand up for myself."

When a couple comes to me to assess whether their marriage dance is complete or in need of transformation from special into soulful, I listen and watch carefully for signs of carelessness, carefulness, or "caringness." Further, I remind the couple that if they are willing to connect their differing values and work together to expose the damaging beliefs and expectations they have each laid upon the other and themselves, the relationship will quickly move back into the caring dynamic.

At this stage, let's explore how Allan's values and mine are connectable, regardless of whether our priorities are similar or not. Allan's current top four priorities are: the success of his truck dealerships; becoming debt-free; renovating; and his fitness level. I know that these are his priorities and values because he spends his resources such as time, money, energy, and effort in attaining them. Most of Allan's waking hours are spent managing his companies, taking trips to Home Depot, going to the gym, and being conscious of saving money.

My top four values are: revealing the innocence and magnificence in people; simplifying my life by downsizing my businesses; writing; and becoming debt-free. The order of each of our values identifies the level of "missingness" where we perceive each value to be, as it is associated with the particular level of mastery we hope to attain. The higher the value is on our list, the more order and organization we will have in that arena. To clarify, I do have a great deal of order, understanding, and knowledge in the area of revealing people's magnificence because I spend so much time in that field in study and observation. However, the level of mastery that I wish to have is still, in my perception, a great distance away. As, in my evaluation, I reach the level of mastery that I am pursuing, revealing people's magnificence will begin to slide down on the values list. This reallocation is definitive of attainment, not appreciation. If my marriage does not show up in the top four of my values, it is only because, in my perception, it is not missing or in jeopardy. If it were, I would certainly raise it to the top.

Now let us consider how Allan's success in his dealerships helps me to reveal the magnificence in people. One way is that Allan employs over 100 people whom I can empower through my coaching business. Another is that through the dealerships and the financial freedom they produce towards our livelihood, I can do pro-bono work for less privileged people, as I see the need, without impacting our own financial obligations. Another connection is that when Allan is doing what he loves all day, it allows me to do what *I* love to do. In addition, the staffs of his dealerships and their extended families offer me the opportunity to attain potential clients. Yet another gain for me is that when Allan is attending to his dealerships, he does not put demands on me to join him in other activities.

Next, let's examine how my pursuit of downsizing my businesses is a benefit to Allan's dealerships. For starters, when I am happy, I place fewer demands on Allan. My downsizing also means fewer financial obligations for me (and us) to worry over. Another gain for his dealerships in my downsizing is that I will have more free time for giving inspirational talks to Allan's management team.

As you can see, the connecting of our differing goals and discussing the empowerment relationship between them has the probable outcome of leaving each of us feeling valued and cared for. When a couple is unaware of such connections, one and often both partners feel unappreciated for what they are pursuing. Identifying and appreciating the couple's differing pursuits are important first steps in evaluating and transforming the relationship.

Alternatively, when a couple has directly opposing key values, the decision to set each other free may be the most loving path the partners can make.

Some time ago, I worked with a couple whose values stood in such strong conflict that they chose the path of marriage completion. Dale was an intern studying to become a plastic surgeon, and Emily was a massage therapist. Dale was trained to believe in science as it applied to healing, while Emily was a deeply searching soul who had studied metaphysics and developed a strong interest in mind/body medicine. The couple's beliefs clashed, however. Emily acknowledged that the traditional medical model had contributed greatly to human health and well-being, but felt strongly that there was much more to be learned on the nonphysical level. Dale took serious issue with this.

Another bone of contention for the pair was the timing of starting their family. Emily wanted to wait no longer than a year after Dale graduated from medical school. Dale wanted to continue studying in the specialty of plastic surgery, particularly in the area of restorative surgery for burn victims, and felt that three years was a more appropriate time frame to aim for. He had promised Emily for years that they would start a family soon. She was now no longer willing to wait—she was 32 and felt her biological clock ticking.

These were the two most obvious differing values and beliefs, although it was evident to me that this couple was in a deeply entrenched power struggle. This was verified for me when I learned that they were sexually intimate only about once a year.

The couple had had a difficult relationship, and there were clear influences of strong archetypal patterns at work. She was the princess looking to be rescued, while he was the burnt-out rescuer and warrior who had been contracted by her soul to teach her to save herself. We discussed this dynamic, and both understood the deeper soul work underway.

After 18 months of deep soul-searching with the intent of identifying their respective wishes and pursuits, it became clear to them that they had accomplished what they had come together to do. In time, Dale had learned that his needs were equally important as the needs of those whom he loved, including Emily and his parents. In his childhood, he had lived a gypsy lifestyle with entrepreneurial parents and often felt abandoned and insecure. His parents had fought often, and though Dale had tried, he had been unable to stop their arguments.

As an adult, he had developed a coping mechanism of verbally minimizing his own needs and desires in order to keep the peace. He made promises he simply could not keep. However, because in his heart he yearned to be a doctor, his needs of studying prevailed over his emotional wish to take care of Emily. Unable to reconcile the two, he eventually suffered an emotional breakdown, and this was a significant wake-up call for him to acknowledge his values and his entitlement to achieving them. This realization was one of the major purposes of his relationship with Emily.

A year following their agreement to complete the marriage, Emily once again fell in love. This time, she paired with a man whose values were closer to her own. She is currently pregnant and glowing! As you can see from this story, relationship success does come in different packages!

In the new paradigm, we understand that we are at times woven together with other people in our life with whom we need to learn and grow in mysterious ways. In addition, we trust that if we commit fully to all of our relationships day by day, they will not compete with one another. Then, gratitude rather than sacrifice will prevail. In the new marriage paradigm, there is no exclusion; there is only an ever-expansive inclusion of all the people and desires that each soul brings to the marriage dance floor.

Remodeling Relationships

Because the foundation of the new paradigm is built upon freedom for, and support of, the individual soul needs for expansion and growth, all events and shadowed beliefs are welcomed and seen as opportunities to expose love. Within the model of a soulful relationship, the couple's needs and wishes are honored and explored for authenticity, and those that are based upon ego are understood as such and released.

The time that it takes to transform the relationship from the old into the new paradigm is of no importance to the couple; the accomplishment of the goal is the focus of this work. For this reason, both mates are aware that their relationship will continue as long as both souls' desires are being communicated with the goal of transforming any beliefs and wishes based upon specialness (lack, autonomy, guilt, possession, fear, and limitation). The couple has therefore agreed to remain paired for as long as the soul-expanding work can be accomplished in the relationship, and to move on when it has been completed. In addition, they agree that at such a time that either party feels that they have completed their soul contract with their partner, they will explore those feelings *to ensure that love and not fear is at their base.* When it is confirmed between the partners that they have completed the contract that their souls came together to do, each agrees to bless the other and gently and caringly remodel the relationship to uphold the other relationships the couple has entered into, such as parenthood.

Because innocence remains the foundation of the relationship, regardless of its transformation from romantic to friendship or parenthood without romantic ties, all the necessary steps are taken to ensure continued caring relationship dynamics. One way in which this is accomplished is in the application of the "Golden Rule," which states, "Do unto others only that which you would have done unto you." If the couple can commit to this one rule, the suffering and heartbreak that typically surround the reframing of marriage into parenthood without romantic ties are avoided.

A second vital step that a couple must take in transiting into the new relationship dance is to promise not to close their hearts to one another. Although this agreement may seem contrary to what our ego wishes us to do as we exit the marriage, it does eliminate the heartache and guilt we normally feel as we depart. This is true because heartache is indicative of the following: We have not expressed all the love and gratitude to our partner that we would have liked to express; we have allowed a fantasy of the future and how long the soul contract should have been, and what acquisitions should have been made before the departure, rule our emotions; and we have begun to close our heart, rather than leave it open, as we remodel our relationship dance. If we ensure that we do not take any of these crippling steps, remodeling can be gentle, loving, and empowering.

The third step we take in remodeling is to agree to keep communicating. The couple must agree that, even as they exit the marriage, there is room for soul growth for both partners. Consequently, each of them agrees to communicate to the other the fears and apprehensions that often accompany life changes. In addition, each party will remind the other that the ongoing "mirroring" of both parties' light and shadow is still underway, and is helpful for both souls to continue to integrate. In fact, with some of the couples beside whom I have walked as they transited into their "new dance," I witnessed that they felt a love for each other that they had never experienced while their relationship was a romantic one.

Chapter Seven

Communication

Everyone knows that communication is vital for ensuring a loving relationship. But what constitutes real communication? I believe that true communication only occurs when we can share our thoughts and feel heard, while being received with all the feelings our perceptions cause to surface, regardless of their validity or origination. When we do not feel safe and received, communication, whether verbal or nonverbal, becomes eclipsed, and will in time recede into resentment. Most of the communication that takes place between people is, in fact, nonverbal; it happens on a thought level. Understanding and learning to listen for the differing thought processes that accompany both communication enhancement and communication breakdown are important steps in creating a soulful, rather than special, relationship.

The Macro-Self vs. the Ego-Self

In conversations, there are two sides to the thought process that evokes the words we say. On one side of the conversation model are ideas, beliefs, and orientations that facilitate strength; and on the other side are ideas, beliefs, and assumptions that give rise to weakness. Having the two sides at work establishes an opportunity to shed away our ego identities, thus revealing our true selves. This is accomplished through choosing communication based on love, rather than fear.

The "strength" side is connected to our authentic self. It nurtures unity-orientated recognition and empowerment. Conversely, on the opposite side of the model is the ego-orientated thought process, which focuses on self-absorption and weakness. As we converse, there is a natural movement between the two identities we embrace—the authentic self and the ego self. These opposing selves can be recognized in the language that we use when we speak—how we communicate—particularly in our tone of voice, energy, and body language.

Defensiveness in tone or action is a sure sign that the person is identifying with the ego instead of their authentic self, and their language will mirror that. Since each self speaks from differing ideologies— either fear or love—yet wishes to express itself in order to feel heard and appreciated, we can train ourselves to hear with "whom" we are speaking at any given time in our conversation. Accordingly, if we wish to encourage the recovery of the authentic self, we need to learn the art of identifying each self as it emerges in both our mate and ourselves.

Soul growth is synonymous with the surrendering of the partners' egos. Therefore, to enhance conversation and create true communication, it is imperative to understand the ego's need to be right, its desire to blame others, its obsession with control, and its fixation with being autonomous and intensely defensive. Defensiveness erupts whenever we feel exposed, revealing our unloved parts and behaviors, and our young emotional self. This emotional "child" that we all have within us has formulated certain beliefs, based on its limited awareness or perceptions. In short, the child-self is terrified of being wrong and being abandoned or rejected. It is encouraging to know that we can learn to speak in ways that nurture the authentic self rather than the wounded ego persona in one another. This is the goal towards which we need to work.

When we identify ourselves as the ego-self, we are self-absorbed, limited, and defensive, and in this condition we cannot communicate—we can only become withdrawn, and dictate or humiliate. In fact, in this state of being, we can't fully hear the other person; we can only extract limited information—that which supports us in our idea of being victimized and powerless.

When we are aligned with our macro-self, however, we are able to hear fully, because we are in a state of authentic power. From this position, we are listening to our partner with compassion and with recognition that everything they are saying is also true for us in some area of our life. We are listening for our own fears and apprehensions, acknowledging the sameness between our partner and us, rather than trying to be better than them. It is fair to say, then, that equality is a foundational brick of communication.

Since the macro-self is our natural state of being, we strive in our conversations to elicit this macro-self from our mate in hopes of healing the joint wounds that we share. In soulful relationships, we bring into the open all the ideas, memories, fears, and hurts that sustain the ego identities, in order to enable their transformation from fear and specialness to love and inclusiveness. When we hear our mate conversing through the ego identity, we first acknowledge how they must be feeling by repeating back to them what they just said. We continue to do this until they can "hear themselves" and recognize which self is directing their words. We do this in an attitude of love with the intention of moving the conversation forward.

In truth, we always yearn to be in contact with our authentic self. So, if we are patient because we are certain that our mate is searching for, and has access to, their authentic self, we become conduits of transformation. From doing this mirroring work, we realize that we, too, are being given an opportunity to support our authentic self. Therefore, gratitude, rather than the resentment that often accompanies a breakdown in communication, emerges within our being. With our shift in awareness and the ownership of our macro-self, disempowered language swiftly shifts to words that reflect empowerment, appreciation, and love.

As the listener within the conversation, we have a crucial function, and one which I believe to be the most important work framing the transformative model of communication. It is imperative for the listener to hold an attitude of *certainty*. When we find ourselves in a situation where communication has shut down, our function is to hold in mind with certainty that our partner is spirit, not ego, and innocent, rather than guilty. Most importantly, we must know that their being is at the effect of love, not fear. When conversations get "bumpy," it is vital that we recognize that unconscious withdrawal from communication is always directed by the ego—the wounded and emotionally immature self. Subsequently, an invitation to our mate to return to the conversation once they are feeling safe and completely received with all their emotions (positive and negative), can be liberating for the couple. If we truly want honest communication, we will also need to receive our partner's shadow sides, knowing that we, too, have a shadow side that we want embraced.

From this position, we can ask our partner questions that nurture their identification with their authentic self, rather than their ego-self. We can ask questions such as: Do you want to talk with me so that we can both feel connected to one another again? Are you feeling empowered right now or powerless? What are you afraid of losing, and can I help you to reclaim it? What can I do to support the authentic self within you *now*? Would saying I am sorry help? Can you try to remember that the past does not have to dictate how you want to feel now? Do you know that no matter what you say or do, I will still love and appreciate you?

Each of these questions provides an opportunity to reclaim birthrights such as peace of mind, appreciation, gratitude, power, freedom, expansiveness, and the full encompassment of our authentic selves.

Communication is synonymous with love. Communication is an act of communion, which is sharing to maintain equality. Accordingly, both love and communication must be extended in order to exist. Love is an idea, as all things are ideas.

Everything in form began as a thought and must be sustained by a thought.[5] If the thought (a belief or desire) is abandoned because we no longer believe it to be true, the form will disappear. The "extension" attributes of love and thought are synonymous in that when an idea is shared, all of it remains with the giver, even though all of it is also given away. Thus, each time we share an idea, we increase it in doing so. If we share the idea of soulful love, it will increase each time another individual adopts the paradigm as congruent with their heart's desire.

The law of giving and receiving states that both actions are the same in value and will produce gain for both giver and receiver. All ideas are governed by this law, which applies to thoughts that are natural expressions of love, as well as to those that are not. In particular, we need to recognize that thoughts that are derived from the desire for specialness (autonomy, guilt, shame, fear, being better than, being right) increase with sharing as well.

When we identify ourselves as special—the ego— we create a relationship that supports that "special" self, and our conversations move away from macro-self recognition and empowerment to micro-self, self-absorption, and weakness. In that state, we are defensive, shut down, and, more often than not, become deaf to the feelings and position of our mate.

We are always communicating, even when we are not verbalizing, because mind is shared by all of humanity. The fear and unrest that arise from the idea of sharing one mind are indicative of the deeply

---

[5] Please refer to my book *Rediscovering Your Authentic Self* for more information on this topic.

buried feelings of guilt we hold in our consciousness. Guilt arose when we thought we could turn away from love by adopting the idea of specialness. Subsequently, we have learned to connect the idea of sharing one mind with that of transparency. Since we do not want the hidden thoughts produced by the ego to be known to others, and because the ego tells us that there is a wretched guilt within us for choosing specialness over love and private thoughts over transparent unified ones, the open sharing of our mind is then associated with vulnerability, which in ego terms means powerlessness and weakness. The ego mind then deduces that transparency of mind implies the exposing of the self that we authentically are. Because we could not, nor ever actually did, usurp love, our natural being remains intact. The ego is indeed afraid of our true loving radiance, and it knows that when we find this authentic self in ourselves and in each other, the ego will cease to exist. It is for this reason that it maintains the urgency for us to keep private thoughts alive. In so doing, however, we sustain special rather than soulful relationships.

Transparent communication is like a light that illuminates the darkness. Darkness simply vanishes into the nothingness from which it arose. The ego is not interested in any conversation that has as its goal the abolishment of guilt and the reinstatement of innocence; however, the authentic self within us certainly is.

The ego whispers that there are horrid facets in our nature that must remain hidden. It instills within us the belief that if our partners saw or knew of these thoughts, they would run away in disgust. It warns us to keep a part of us away, especially any part that would expose us as being vulnerable. In our conversations, we are directed to never expose our mistakes or ego-orientated words and actions, since they will perpetuate the already heavy burden of guilt we are carrying. By listening to the whispers of the ego and by keeping private thoughts, we sabotage the awareness of the unassailable innocence we share.

Soulful conversations, on the other hand, are based on a shared innocence and the mutual desire to expose and heal all thoughts and perceptions based on fear, lack, or loss. The discussions are directed by the spirit, not the ego, and are customized to reveal magnificence, not limit or loss. In a soulful relationship, neither party wishes to blame the other for difficulties they are enduring together. Rather, each soul identifies the ways in which the situation can be used to advance their soul growth, since both realize that they are indeed reflections of one another. From this perspective, all healing work is mutually beneficial, and is looked forward to, rather than avoided.

Sharing Secrets

In this section, I wish to explore the concept of ideas, thoughts, and actions that we want to keep secret because we would feel mortified if our mate knew about them. Secrets that are connected to acts of infidelity are addressed in chapter eight, *The Question of Fidelity*.

Secrets begin to exist when we believe that we would lose something of real value to us if certain information were exposed. Further, secrets are kept hidden from one another when we associate the exposure of the secret with feelings of shamefulness that we would have to endure if a thought, a desire, a past action, or a currently contemplated action were to be revealed. Compounding the fear yet further is the thought of looking foolish, naïve, desperate, stupid, or careless in the eyes of our mate, or even our own. We are therefore terrified of having our weaknesses exposed, and, in particular, are invested in hiding any actions that, in our quest for validation, appreciation, and increased self-worth, we have participated in.

The sharing of secrets can be a deeply healing and connective act for a couple if they can assure each other that no matter what is said, they will just listen with a compassionate and open heart. Secrets are crippling to soulful love because they support the malignant belief that there is some part of us that is unworthy of love.

In working with couples, I give them the exercise of sharing secrets, usually beginning with the least scary one, and working their way up. To the couples' surprise and amazement, however, the partners often realize that the secrets are either not really secrets, or that they are not unlike secrets that the other also harbors.

Secrets of sexual desires that an individual wishes to have explored or fulfilled can be liberating and help to remove the sexual blocks the pair may be enduring. The promise on the part of the secret holder to the mate to move as slowly as the most apprehensive partner wants to move ensures confidence in traveling down these uncharted waters, and will often build intimacy not only sexually, but on many other levels as well.

Nurturing Intimacy

The soul yearns for moments of intimacy. And the authentic self within us all is magnetically drawn towards any opportunity to be intimate, not just physically, but emotionally and communicatively as well. Through the act of intimacy, we are unveiled, revealing our unprotected, unlimited, and unbounded radiant self. For this reason, intimacy is the dance of the soul, yet sheer treachery to the ego.

Intimacy occurs whenever we are courageous enough to dissolve our protective boundaries—any time we are not consumed with the desire to be better than another. It occurs in any instant we choose the position of vulnerability over being defensive. In the decision to be intimate, we choose our macro–identification, rather than the micro-self. We override the need for control and protectiveness, and instead choose transparency and openheartedness.

The courage to be intimate comes from changing our belief and from understanding that transparency and vulnerability do not equate to a threat of injury or loss to our real self. Intimacy is not a show of weakness, nor indicative of a powerless person. Rather, it is a sure indication of an emotionally matured, integrated personality.

Our socially programmed idea that intimacy is to be experienced only with those safest or closest to us is in need of change. Because intimacy is a violation to the ego, both individually and collectively, strides taken towards its accomplishment will require patience and compassion. Because the very idea of intimacy is a threat to our ego persona and thus our autonomous self, we spend more time avoiding intimacy than embracing it. The truth is that we can be intimate with everyone all of the time, if we truly understand what intimacy is.

To be intimate with another means to be willing to set aside our need to have power over another person, and to share our fullness—our shadow and light sides. It means breaking social, religious, and ethnically constructed rules which are meant to separate us from one another. These are rules that are meant to uphold private thoughts and desires, personal information and orientations, and, in particular, any mistakes we may have made.

Being intimate takes courage because it will usually feel uncomfortable at first to bust the rules. The rewards are well worth the effort, though, if we can allow the emerging feelings of foolishness, vulnerability, and transparency to act as a salve upon our parched souls, which hunger for intimacy's nurturing.

Many people say that it is necessary for us to place boundaries around ourselves in order not to be violated, abused, or taken advantage of. I do not subscribe to that belief. From my observation, we need more surrendering of boundaries than building them. When we have the courage to be ourselves transparently, unveiling our vast emotions which encompass both the shadow and light sides of our humanness, we will, in turn, finally be able to receive ourselves and each other that way, too.

I do believe that the Great Wall of China, the Berlin Wall, and the fences we place around our hearts and properties, as well as all the "rules" that are also meant to keep us away or separated from one another, are reflections of the ego mind, which is committed to that goal. The outer walls are nothing more than an outpicturing of the inner fear of unity, equality, being seen, or taken advantage of.

One way that we can begin to lead more intimate lives is by asking better questions—questions that offer up the opportunity to reveal what inspires us, makes us smile, or causes us to be sad. As a baby step towards that goal, next time you are at the checkout counter, try *not* saying to the checkout person, "Hi, how are you?" when you don't plan to really listen for the answer. Instead, try looking at them while searching for their best feature, and then compliment them on it. Or compliment them on being very fast or caring. Try asking them *if they are having a great day.* All of these are small acts of intimacy, because they are looking more deeply into the other person in hopes of connecting and merging, even if only for an instant. We are so hypnotized into shallowness, but intimate act by intimate act, we become more comfortable with intimacy and eventually begin to crave it in all our encounters.

Before we can hope to have intimacy with our mate physically, we need to establish emotional and spiritual intimacy. We will only share ourselves with those with whom we feel equality and with whom we feel safe, and by whom we are not criticized or unappreciated.

Whenever we begin to harbor feelings of anger, hurt, or resentment that we are unwilling to discuss, the erosion of intimacy begins. The by-product of our silence will in time become the need or desire for a wall or boundary around us. In reality, what we are saying to our mate is, "You have hurt me in some way, and so I do not want you to have an open invitation to my body." We punish one another by withholding ourselves in various ways. Some withhold words; others withhold their body. I do both. No matter how much work we have done to cultivate intimacy in our relationship, if we start holding on to, rather than expressing, our hurts and resentments, our walls will go up. Over years, this resentment will extinguish the fire between the couple.

This scenario played out in an incident between Allan and me a few years ago. (Although it occurred long before my frank discussion with him, described in chapter four, about the lack of fire I felt for him, it could repeat at any time at which resentment is allowed to poison the relationship.) One evening, Allan was "spooning" me in bed with his hand cupped around my breast. He loved to let his hand "dance" over my body, and at times I hated it. I felt violated and resentful; feelings of rage would come over me, and I told him that I felt he was overstepping my comfort zone. He felt emotionally "slapped" by my response.

Years had gone by without my ever mentioning how I was feeling about his advances. The whisper of the ego said, "If you tell him how you are feeling, he will feel rejected, and you will be seen as cruel." Time after time, I silenced my words, as my emotions screamed, "Don't touch me!"

My silence was a by-product of the rage and feeling of violation I had been swallowing for years, and which was swiftly eroding my desire for intimacy. Any yearning I may have felt in my soul towards achieving an intimate union was being suffocated by the anger I was harboring inside for countless infractions of which I was unwilling to let go. I had deduced correctly that the letting go of the hurts of the past couple of years would have paved the way back into our oneness. I also knew that there was still a strong ego-pull within me that wanted to make Allan suffer for a myriad of things, such as being mean to my kids, being aloof, controlling me with his money, always needing to be right, and so on. I realized that for these things I wanted him to suffer as I had suffered, more than I wanted to set him (and thus us) free. Consequently, the ego was winning in its quest to block intimacy in our relationship. I did not recognize this at first.

Then, through my deeper yearning for truth and honesty, and by asking myself the right questions, I realized that by not telling Allan of my personal boundaries, I was doing more damage than I could possibly have done by sharing.

The ego often tells us to be silent rather than communicative, in hopes of creating enough pent-up rage so that we will eventually blow up, saying or doing something that we will deeply regret later. Recognizing this, I decided to share.

My heart pounded in my throat, and tears rolled down my face as I shared with Allan that I often sat in the bathroom crying because of the trespasses I felt he had done. Allan lay silent—yet I felt his pain filling my heart, his emotions coursing through my veins.

"How did we get here?" I wondered. I knew that his soul hungered for my being more than for my body. I knew that all of us have at times misinterpreted the yearning for physical intimacy in that way. He was innocent, as was I, and he only interpreted his hunger in the ways he had been conditioned and hypnotized to do, just as I had been hypnotized into the belief that I needed boundaries.

Then, with gentleness, he stated, "I thought we had paralleled our paths to eliminate boundaries and separations—to experience our oneness? I thought we were moving ever closer towards intimacy, acceptance, and freedom? I think you are afraid of intimacy, just like me!"

Wham!—his words echoed through my whole being, stringing together lifetimes of fear, as if they were pearls. He was right; I was terrified of intimacy, but not with my clients or friends—I had overcome that fear long ago. No, I was terrified of intimacy with Allan. "He is my other self," I thought. Dancing intimately with him, melting all my protective boundaries with him, being transparent with him, merging with him, somehow, magically, allowed me to own myself completely.

I suddenly awakened to the remembrance that intimacy was the dance of divine love, the kissing of the face of God. In an instant that felt like eternity, I was being offered the opportunity to be my authentic and innocent self, as well as feel all that I had been terrified to feel, yet pained for.

It always astonishes me how our fears *are the dragons* protecting *our deepest treasures*. I realized that I had gone numb some time ago, and the tingling, like that which occurs when our leg wakes up after we have pinched off the blood supply, hurt.

I have concluded that intimacy is something we both ache for and are terrified of. This is so because we have correctly associated intimacy with the loss of our individualized self. Gratefully, however, when we engage in acts of intimacy, what rushes to meet us instead of loss is a more authentic identity. Frailty and smallness are exchanged for strength, expansiveness, and that experience we so crave—transparent love!

Chapter Eight

The Question of Fidelity

This chapter is a bit like a puzzle—there are many "pieces" to consider in this often fragile and thought-provoking topic. It is written with the hope that it can help individuals to survive infidelity in a relationship. It is also an exploration of what fidelity means, with reflection upon the greater purpose of this book, which is to embrace a more mindful, and soulful, relationship.

Emotional Hunger and Infidelity

The topic of fidelity has been both a gift and a challenge for me to ponder and write about. It brought with it a great deal of reflection on the truest and deepest meaning of love. Love and commitment seem to be synonymous, but the deeper question is: To *what* is love committed? The answer may vary for each of us, but what is certain is that the question itself will unveil the differing objectives of the ego and spirit—the primary consideration of this chapter.

In my exploration of this subject and the many related angles to be considered, I discovered that infidelity is always linked to a search for something that we feel is missing, or to a desire to have more of something that we feel is of value. Our hunger to have the "something" that we believe to be missing, or possess *more of* what we think would fulfill us, is the driving force behind fidelity.

The numerous things that we desire and that we believe would increase our sense of self and happiness become *idols* which include attention, power, sexual fire, intimacy, more money, social influence, good looks, and so on. Hunger arises within us whenever we regard ourselves as being limited or as being a body instead of an unbounded, abundant, and all-encompassing spirit who *uses a body*. Idols are the external manifestations that represent the ego idea of wanting and being *more of,* and *better than,* anything or anyone else. *More of,* and *better than,* can be applied to things related to either pleasure or pain. For the ego, it is irrelevant if the "more of" desire aims to embrace more sorrow, more heartbreak, more loss, more cruelty, more or less money, better cars, a better body, more intelligence, better friends, or a better job...as long as we feel we are "special" in that we are not equal to another.

We have collectively been hypnotized into believing that our attainment and *securing* of the things on the list will make us "happier." Look closely and you will realize that the list itself is indicative of our deeply seated belief that we are not already abundant and without lack of any kind. And what is eclipsed in this searching is that as we search, we disinherit the truth that we *are* already magnificent and equal to everyone else. Our essence is the same as that of everyone around us, and it is only when we forget this that we hunger for anything at all. Since no one "out there" can really provide us with anything we do not already have hidden within us, we need not search outside of ourselves for that which we hunger for.

What is deemed by the soul as being valuable, and is of authentic eternal value, is anything that increases by being given away. For instance, if you share an idea with someone, all of the idea remains yours, while at the same time, all of it is being given away. The idea is shared and is increased by the number of people who accept the idea. This is also true of the sharing of love, kindness, truth, and knowledge.

Therefore, since infidelity and the idea of lack or specialness are inseparable, accepting one's completeness and fullness is the first step to take if we want to remain faithful.

My reflections on fidelity have demanded of me the assessment of which *self* we identify with, and therefore aim to protect through being faithful. In these pages, fidelity will be explored not only in sexual terms involving our mate, but also in its most expansive expressions, including fidelity to the self, and, in particular, to love.

I have examined the purpose and the often overemphasized importance of the body, and the minimization of the significance of the soul in monogamous relationships. I have investigated the desire for security as it applies to the support of our physical needs, which include food, shelter, and financial stability.

Further, I have examined the human evolutionary process—our journey from the time when we secured our basic needs while living in caves to our current era—considering at length the differing needs we had as we collectively grew in reasoning ability and intelligence. Consequently, I have taken into account what rules and boundaries we may have needed to ensure survival early on in our development. A question to consider is, will we always need these boundaries, or will we mature beyond them?

Two Identities—Two Sets of Rules

As previously discussed, we each have two concepts of self: One is our real self, the macro-self, based upon our authentic identity as an unbounded spirit that is loving, abundant, and without lack or need of any kind. The other concept of self is the micro-self, which emerges whenever we deny our macro-self identification.

It would be accurate to say that the micro-self is the shadow of our authentic macro-self. The micro-self is afraid because it does realize, however dimly, that it is not what it pretends to be. Afraid of becoming exposed as an impostor, it is defensive and protective. The micro-self believes it is under attack and is lacking something, and it is in constant pursuit of attaining the perceived void. The micro-self is indeed lacking "something"; this something is the realization of the truth of its identity. The illusory micro-self emerges in any moment we deny our spiritual essence. Therefore, it approaches life and the human experiences we encounter in ways that are diametrically opposed to those of the macro-self.

Since the subject of fidelity has caused me to search so earnestly within my belief systems to determine which "self" abides by which "rules," I thought it was important to explore how each self approaches the subject. I have concluded that my micro-self wants "stuff"—safety, security, assurances, guarantees, and rewards in order to be willing to participate in the romantic dance at all. And I realized that I had imposed "rules" based on fear (lack) upon previous relationships because I was afraid of losing what I valued. I demanded fidelity because of my fear of losing the "things" that made me feel safe. The list included the things that I had decided would uphold some form of "ego esteem." The things I needed to feel secure included a "perfect" family model, the "perfect" marriage, physical possessions such as money, investments, furnishings, real estate, a car, a motorcycle, and so on. These were the things or "idols" I felt in jeopardy of losing.

Through a magnified look at the reasons why I wanted faithfulness from my husbands, it was revealed to me that I had seen fidelity as a type of "insurance package." Fidelity could help me protect what I felt was mine; it made me feel that it was safe to love.

Since this discovery years ago, I have engaged in countless discussions about fidelity with couples, clients, friends, and students, as well as with Allan, and realized that I was not alone in my attempt to understand the foundation of fidelity. The couples with whom I discussed this subject agreed that most of the rules of fidelity are indeed set up to govern and place boundaries around our mate's actions, so that we can feel more secure, loved, and valued. They also agreed, however, that there are other important reasons why fidelity is coveted—needs that are not physically driven.

The "fidelity policy" is aimed at ensuring safety for our overall well-being, which includes our emotions and sense of self. The act of faithfulness is directed towards supporting our self-esteem and our physical, psychological, and emotional needs. But it also does something else of equal importance: Fidelity facilitates the groundwork that enables us to feel secure enough to be intimate with another soul.

Evolving through Love

In our agreement to be faithful, we do show our mate our care, commitment, and love, don't we? I believe the answer to be both yes and no, depending on the maturity of our love. The question I pose is: Is there a deeper level to love—the love that I have been referring to as *soulful love*—that is unbounded and ungoverned by any rules? And if so, is there an evolutionary process that takes us to the ability to love this freely, intimately, openly, and transparently? Is soulful love accomplished by moving through two stages of selfhood and thus love? I believe so.

I believe that the climb to soulful love must be accomplished first through the full embrace and integration of *human love*, which evolves out of the "special" relationship that is always based on guilt, lack, and separation. Human love emerges when we transcend our need to support guilt, be needed instead of wanted, and remain separate within our relationships. Soulful love finally arises when we are able to have full commitments to all relationships simultaneously. With soulful love comes the absolute belief in innocence and unification, as well as an understanding that relationships do not compete. To the ego, this idea is ludicrous. The following is a detailed description of the three stages of love.

Soulful Love
(2nd stage)

Human Love
(1st stage)

Special Relationship
(based on fear and guilt)

Special Relationship: Fear-based thinking; presumed guilt; feelings of lack, unworthiness; co-dependent, autonomous behaviors and low self-esteem; judgment, denial, and avoidance of the shadow side of the personality.

Human Love: Presumed equality; self-esteem; self-acceptance; feeling worthy, lovable, independent; holding a "we" mentality; altruistic behavior; owning and appreciating both the light and shadow sides of personality.

Soulful Love: Unbounded love; transparent, omnipresent, intimate, vulnerable, unassailable, protected innocence; spaceless and timeless, interdependent, creative; full integration of personality; only light emanates with feelings of joy and appreciation.

The first stage of love, which I identified above as being human love, is the care we show through recognizing that our mate's needs are as important as ours. It is the connecting of our values and desires, and the acknowledgment that both souls' needs are equally important. Prior to this stage is the "special" relationship, which again, *is not based on love at all*, rather it is based on fear and the belief that we are autonomous, guilty, lacking, and unlovable. It is founded on the presumption that the only way to get what we feel is missing in us is to take it from another!

Stage-one love (human love) includes the care and attention, appreciation, and the integration of all of our spouse's and our own shadow and light sides. Human love is based upon our growing self-awareness. The human love model meets the differing and changing values and needs of a couple. Stage-one love presides when we have sufficiently grown in our self-esteem to appreciate, acknowledge, and honor all traits and sides of our partner and ourselves.

Human love grows and ultimately is transcended to become soulful love, much as adolescence is transcended into adulthood. Human love is transcended once we have learned to love and appreciate all people's (including our own) total natures.

To illustrate the ideas introduced here, I will share the story of a couple I worked with years ago who were struggling with infidelity in their relationship. At the time of our initial meeting, their relationship was at the "special" stage.

Kate, who was in her early thirties, was a devoted stay-at-home mom and spiritual seeker. Her husband, Dale, was a 40-year-old electrical engineer. Kate had worked with me for several years before infidelity struck their relationship. She and Dale had been together for 18 years. They had three children, the youngest of whom was 9 years old at the time of the affair.

Kate and Dale shared one top value—the welfare of their kids. They also both enjoyed playing sports and staying fit. But their values diverged on spiritual issues. Dale had no inclination to pursue spirituality, whereas Kate held the search for God highly in her values. Dale minimized all efforts she made towards that goal. Dale valued money. He was also a "controller," monitoring Kate's every movement and every dollar that she spent. As a result, Kate began to hide her spending to minimize Dale' angry outbursts. Neither person really worked on keeping friendship alive within their marriage; rather, they had defaulted to basic "survival mode." Dale had lost his passion in many areas of life, including his work, the care of their home, and their marriage. Kate was the opposite; she was passionate about their home, their kids' happiness, her fitness level, and her personal growth and development. Both Kate and Dale were starving for intimacy on all levels. During the sessions that Kate and I had together, our discussions often turned to the question of *why she was choosing* to be with someone so controlling of her every move.

Dale and Kate arrived in my office, following a call I made to Dale in response to Kate's tear-filled confession of the affair. She disclosed that Dale had found out about the affair, and had taken away the car keys and threatened to change the locks on the house. Kate was terrified of what Dale might do next; she suspected he would take the kids away from her. At Kate's request, I called him. He was in shock, deeply hurt and afraid, and wanted some understanding of how this could have happened to him. I asked him to come in with her, so we could get clarity about the situation. He agreed.

Dale had discovered that Kate was having an affair when he searched for the car keys one day. While reaching into her coat pocket, he found a note which read, "Hey, Sexy, see you tonight at 7. Wear black; miss you already." Dale immediately confronted Kate about this note, and she confessed to the affair.

Kate shared that she had quite innocently begun flirting with a neighbor a year previously, and things eventually got out of hand. She also stated that she was confused, but felt that she was definitely finished with her marriage. She said she was tired of being controlled and always being criticized for something. She was fed up with being patronized and being treated like a little girl. Dale was clinging to the chair's armrest, with tears in his eyes; he begged me to help them.

I began by telling them that the affair was not the real reason they were on such fragile ground; rather, the reason was their inability to communicate and be honest with each other. I knew that this marriage was in trouble because I recognized that Kate was growing into a better sense of self, which would not tolerate being oppressed.

With Dale present, I asked Kate how long she had been starving for intimacy, to which she replied that she had felt this way for the last ten years. She told Dale that he was self-absorbed and selfish. Dale always came first! Dale nodded in agreement. I asked Dale if he knew that he was partially responsible for Kate's having the affair. He looked at me in bewilderment.

I explained to the couple that when we are emotionally hungry and are not fed, we will eventually find someone or something to feed us. For Kate, her spiritual pursuits had been satisfying a part of that hunger, but as she grew in self-love as a result of her growth, she hungered for believing in her worthiness even more. And through that desire for more, she eventually became very susceptible to another man's advances of interest, since her husband showed so little.

I shared with them that if Kate's top values included being spiritual, feeling valued, being seen as intelligent, feeling cared for, being viewed as pretty and desirable, and Dale was unwilling or unable to provide or support those needs, the marriage was destined for completion. Dale said that he understood and would do anything to get her back. Kate was un-moved by his words. In that moment, she clearly felt that she was finished.

I asked her if she had considered the impact of a divorce on her kids, to which she replied that she had done this and concluded that in the current situation, her children were getting a warped view of what a marriage was.

Kate then pulled out a list of reasons why she felt that the marriage was over. This list included Dale's being a control freak, grumpy, selfish, self-absorbed, hating Kate's spirituality, and hating dancing. Dale said he was willing to change.

We agreed that they needed some space to sort through the flood of feelings that were drowning the marriage. They agreed to live apart for the next few days—Kate and the kids stayed with her mother. I asked the couple to see me individually first and then to return together in a few days, so that we could delve more deeply into the issues. I also assured them that their old marriage was over and a new one could begin if they were both willing to take some responsibility for their situation.

Now let's learn a little more about the topic of fidelity, and then we will get back to Dale and Kate's story.

Morals, Values, Traits, and Beliefs

Differences in values and morals between cultures and societies are evident. What one group sees as an act of love may be judged by another group as being cruel and unimaginable. These often conflicting ideas have created wars and immeasurable human suffering over the ages. The beliefs of the different religions and denominations of the people in the Middle East make this point crystal clear. We set up differing moral and tribal rules to protect what we value and what we consider as being in jeopardy of loss. We enact differing rituals based on our varied beliefs, and often they are founded on religious tenets.

Even our sexual orientations and accepted behaviors vary. Female circumcision, for instance, is clearly considered perverse and cruel in North America, but it is widely practiced in several African countries. Another example of poignant clarity is found in a prenuptial ritual that is practiced among certain tribes in Africa. On the night before the wedding, the parents of the bride and groom celebrate the children's move into married life. As part of the celebration, the bride will spend time alone with her father, where she is free to ask questions, touch, and be touched to prepare her for her groom. The same is done with the groom and his mother. The tribe's belief is that it is the parents' final duty to prepare their child for sexual intimacy with their spouse. This ritual is revered as one of the holiest, most beautiful expressions of love between the child and his or her parent. In North America, we would consider this practice perverse, and pursue legal action against the individuals involved.

Another values-based behavior, albeit a less dramatic example, is the practice of smoking cigarettes. In the 1950s, smoking was posh, sexy, and glamorous, and many movie stars were seen smoking on the screen. Now, we would rise up in anger if we were to see cigarettes advertised to young people.

Currently, many cultures differ considerably in their beliefs and approaches to sexuality and their evaluation of the "good" and "bad" activities, qualities, and rituals. In every culture, and since the early days of human consciousness, values and beliefs have changed to accommodate the differing goals of each society. As members of a particular culture, we adopt the existing cultural rules, and we also create some of our own.

We could ask ourselves whether our understanding of fidelity is also subject to such an evolutionary process.

Over time in our evolution, we grew in self-awareness and began to unfold more and more traits, both positive and negative, to support the differing needs of life. We also needed to ensure safety in the spiritual, familial, tribal, social, and financial arenas, and therefore rules were implemented to help us protect what was valuable.

As we continued to evolve, our evaluations based upon whatever the "tribe" considered to be "missing" or in short supply (food, shelter, security, enough men to hunt, and women to raise the young) continued to change. Through this, and because of our ego's desire for approval and our desperate wish to be evaluated as "good," we began a continuous process of striving. As this process unfolded, there simultaneously arose an increased awareness of our need for, and our worthiness of, love. The link between security and love was established, and this link continues to evolve us, bringing with it deeper questions.

For Kate, traveling along this evolutionary process meant that she began to value, and thus want to protect, her own sense of equality in the relationship. She realized she deserved as much respect, adoration, and financial freedom as she perceived Dale to have. And she was willing to *unconsciously* push the marriage into a crisis to either get her desires met or to get out of the marriage to achieve these wants.

I met with Dale the day after our first meeting because I wanted to focus on his emotional needs and wounds. I began by empathizing with his pain and shared that I, too, had experienced firsthand how devastating it feels to discover that one's spouse is having an affair. I also told him that years later, after much reflection on the experience and an evaluation of all that I have learned about myself from it, I would not trade it for anything. Dale asked what it was that I had learned. First, I shared that in my heart I knew that my relationship with my first husband had been largely based on lack, fear, and need, rather than on love, which encompasses transparency, abundance, and completeness. I also shared that, since I had been "betrayed," I knew that there was some need my former spouse had which he felt I was either unable or unwilling to fill. Most important, however, was that in my heart, I recognized that I had been betraying and minimizing myself, and my ex-husband was mirroring that to me. I shared that I had been aware of the fact that my ex-husband really wanted to be with another woman, but instead of honoring that realization, I stayed, and in so doing, I was really betraying my own heart's desire to love and be loved equally.

Dale sat speechless, with a deep look of understanding in his eyes that reflected his inner wisdom. He then asked if I really believed it was possible to "win" Kate back. I said if it was for the highest good of both souls, he could, but if not, the answer was no. However, I assured him that either way, he would be transformed by the experience, and if he could remain open to growing and changing his fear-based views and beliefs, the payoff would be worth the pain he had experienced.

Later that day, I spoke with Kate on the phone. She was still feeling overwhelmed and overshadowed with guilt, confusion, and fear, and she shared that if she did not get out of the marriage now, she feared she would never again find the courage to do so. I promised her that the decision to go or stay in the marriage needed to be made through love, not fear, and I assured her that together, we could make sure that her decision would be love-based.

The next day, I visited again with Dale and Kate, and we explored what it would take for Kate to be willing to reconsider her plans for divorce. She could not think of anything. I offered her the idea that since she was a spiritual seeker and in pursuit of God, which meant that she sought to understand love, the affair could be used as a "workbook" towards such a goal. This got her attention, because I had spoken to her in her values system. Dale appeared afraid at this suggestion because of his lack of understanding of Kate's pursuits. It was clear to me that Kate's wisdom in this arena of life aroused in him two powerfully disabling emotions: feeling stupid and out of control.

I assured Dale that I was not interested in converting him towards becoming spiritually driven, although Kate said that *she* was!

I asked Dale what he knew about Kate's spiritual pursuits. He replied that he knew nothing about them. I asked him if he believed in a higher power or intelligence. He said that he did, and this provided us with a brick to build upon. I asked Kate to share with Dale the reasons why she pursued God, and what a spiritually focused life meant to her. Kate replied that she had gained more self-appreciation, patience, compassion, understanding, and tolerance from her spiritual studies and practices. Dale listened, nodding in agreement with much of what Kate shared. Kate added that she had become much less judgmental, less defensive, and was more at peace, because she did not feel the need to control so many things around her. Dale got the message! When Kate was finished, Dale disclosed that he, too, wanted to feel the things Kate had said she was getting from her pursuit.

Next, we began to discuss how Kate had fallen into the affair, and I asked her to give as many details of the encounters as possible, so that Dale could begin to let go of the fantasies he was conjuring up about what may have happened. Kate hesitantly agreed, provided that Dale would not keep interrupting her and argue with her on the facts. He agreed to remain quiet. I offered him a note pad to write down questions that arose, and that he could ask Kate to address at the end of her sharing.

Kate described each encounter, disclosing as many details as she could remember. There had been 13 interludes over a one-year period. Kate's disclosure of the circumstances of the encounters between herself and Phil were like pieces of a puzzle that Dale began to put into place. Following Kate's sharing and some follow-up questions posed by Dale pertaining to certain events that transpired when Kate was absent from their home, the room fell silent. Gently, I again brought into their awareness that it was largely Kate's emotionally based hunger for values and self-worth that had fueled the affair. In other words, her desire to feel wanted, needed, sexy, desirable, intelligent, and competent made her susceptible to becoming involved in an affair.

Both Kate and Dale agreed with this deduction, yet Kate still felt deeply wounded and in need of healing and understanding. She addressed Dale and asked him if he realized how much she had wanted him to value her and notice her, not only as the mother of his children, but also for her own sake as a woman and his wife. Remorsefully, Dale began to understand.

As the next step in our work together, I shared with Kate and Dale the driving forces behind the desire for fidelity.

To create a soulful love relationship, we must first learn that any evaluation which condemns another and which is based upon our perception of what is either "good" or "bad" as a trait, rule, action, belief, or thing within others or ourselves is itself an illusion. It is illusory because it is an evaluation based on lack and thus identification with the ego. Since the soulful relationship is founded upon the belief that we are spirit and have an unassailable innocence and perfection beneath the ego coverings, we should allow ourselves to be pardoned, so that we can also pardon others for their mistakes.

I shared with Dale and Kate that they would both need to embark upon a *selective remembering* process if they wanted to heal. I explained that the reality was that it was *only the love that the two shared* which should be remembered and permitted to have a present-day effect on them. Further, they needed to understand that all things said and done by either of them through the micro-self persona or fear could and would eventually need to be pardoned. In addition, they needed to realize that in a soulful relationship, our fluctuating sense of self *is demonstrated* by what we say and do while under the influence of either our spirit (love) or ego (body) identification. And the measuring and punishing of fear-based actions does not mitigate the pain, but love and pardon does. All actions that are the result of our ego identification are based on the idea of lack, and all healing comes from supplying the perceived lack. And since the real self as spirit or love is in need of nothing, the giving of love is *natural*! The ego, on the other hand, is driven by a compilation of perceived lacks and self-infatuations which cannot be fulfilled. We must learn to see all traits and hungers as calls for love, and we must recognize that they represent the move from humanness into divinity and the corresponding change in our understanding of who we are.

Living in the world of duality and being compassionate with our dualistic human nature, which embodies both positive and negative traits and behaviors, is the best we can do when we consider ourselves to be bodies trapped in time and space, and when we are still fluctuating between ego and spirit identification. On the other hand, when we become stabilized in our perception of our authentic self as love and consequently extend only love, we emerge into the second stage of love, which I call soulful or divine love.

Since soulful love has no expectations or limitations—it is love in its deepest expression—it is unassailable and unalterable. It is constant and unified. It can be, and has been, forgotten, but it cannot be obliterated. Soulful love evolves from human love and is the natural expression of our authentic self. It is the love from which we emerged and the love that is expressed between our Creator and ourselves.

Authentic love removes limitations and sets people completely free, placing no expectations on them. Soulful love expands eternally, unencumbered, and unconditioned. It does not look outward for what is within it, because it knows there is nothing outside itself.

When someone is in contact with their authentic self, their self-esteem and authentic self-worth soar. Their spirit and love are unassailable by any action, including what we have called "betrayal" through acts of infidelity. Soulful love is what we all yearn for, and feel magnetized towards.

For Dale and Kate and countless other couples whom I have assisted in transcending betrayal's sting, I needed to discover how we could create this love in our relationships while still needing boundaries around each other's behaviours.

I deduced that if we loved authentically, meaning with complete commitment and adoration of both our mate and ourselves, we would not feel the need to set boundaries around one another. I further concluded that when we love in an authentic fashion, fidelity *is* the by-product of that commitment. For me, as well as for Dale and Kate, the subject of fidelity—and monogamy—has commanded enormous courage and a willingness to be transparent with thoughts, questions, fears, and beliefs. In my quest for answers, I am motivated by a deep desire to grow in my understanding of love and its expansive dynamics. As part of this process, I am willing to be questioned with respect to my moral examinations and my abandoning of boundaries based on fear.

I have openly shared these thought-provoking questions with my husband, close friends, clients, students, and casual acquaintances in order to gather insights from as many people as possible. I admit that I *do not have the one "right answer,"* but I do believe that we each have an answer that resonates with our soul and moral and spiritual fabric.

For Dale and Kate, these deeper questions and the answers that they intuitively felt were right for them, were destined to become vital to their future success. Let's return to their story to see what they discovered.

I asked them both to agree that, for them at the time the acts of infidelity occurred, there was a condition on their love and the relationship. They agreed. I explained that if we say, "I love you provided you…" with an endless and changing list of outcomes or behaviors with which we feel safe, then the love shared between those parties is conditioned. They agreed once more. And, I questioned, if we or our spouse do not comply with the rules and boundaries, will our love wither and die? They both looked puzzled, and then Kate, being a longtime student of *A Course in Miracles*, replied: "If the love dies, it was not really love. It was an arrangement, a special relationship, based on fear." "Yes," I replied. I asked the two of them to seriously think about this, and told Kate that she had been judging Dale as much as he had been controlling her. She had been holding an expectation of how she wanted him to be, rather than loving and appreciating who he was. She nodded. I asked Kate to commit to Dale to do the ongoing work of communicating and understanding what it was that they each had done to bring them to the point where they were today. Kate agreed to remain in the marriage for two more weeks, and to keep searching her heart and mind for the truth.

My research indicates that human love appears to be dependent on rules and behaviors that fluctuate as we feel more or less secure within ourselves. For the purpose of this book, perhaps we could agree that these boundaries may be imperative in the first stages of love, and that they may well build a ladder towards a level where we no longer need them.

I believe that some boundaries are indeed placed in an attempt to make someone feel secure, valued, and cared for, and that fidelity can emerge from love and is aimed at upholding and honoring it.

Yearning for Home

The most compelling spirit-born reason I have found that may be instigating the desire for monogamy in our earthbound relationships is that we inherently crave to replicate our authentic and perfect relationship with the divine. As spiritual beings, in our unalterable relationship with God, I believe we all distantly remember what it is like to experience perfect love—the love expressed between our Creator, the lover, and us, the beloved.

And since the relationship with God is the first relationship that occurred and emerged from love, it seems logical that it was also the perfect template for creating a perfect relationship based *only* on love, trust, faith, and freedom. If indeed it is true that God is love and we were made in love's image, then we are also love. And since we are love, it stands to reason that we would recognize love when it is present, once we had recognized ourselves as the same. From this logical deduction, we can gain insights as to why we yearn so much for love, and are so magnetized towards it.

I have come to *know* that love *is* faithful to *itself*, and through my relationship with this *spirit self*, I have learned a deeper understanding of what love is, and how it sets all things right. Further, it is my belief that it is this ancient memory of divine love that compels us to strive to attain this perfect and complete love here on earth with one another as well. I believed that for Dale and Kate, the desire to know and experience this unconditioned love was as magnetizing as it is for each of us.

A week had passed since Kate and Dale's last session. I had in that time received two phone calls from Kate. In one call she asked if it were really possible that Dale would sustain his newly changing behaviors, and that this might authentically transform their relationship dynamics. I said that I believed so. I also reminded Kate that Dale was her "mirror," and if she had authentically changed, he would, too. In the second call, placed a few hours before their meeting with me, Kate expressed a deep fear that in the future, she would again lose her hard-earned self-esteem. She was concerned that she might never again find the courage to leave Dale if she needed or wanted to. I responded by reminding her that she was also responsible for her deteriorating self-worth because she had not placed herself and her needs parallel to Dale's. I reminded her also that she no longer needed to minimize herself.

In closing, Kate shared that Dale had been asking her to go over the whole story of her infidelity again and again, and she asked me if she should keep doing this. I suggested that we would discuss this question later that day in our session with her and Dale.

Time Passages to Freedom or Guilt

I hung up the phone from Kate, knowing that it was time to review the relationship between time and healing, and how the ego and spirit use time differently. The spirit, which lives in an eternal present moment, never considers past mistakes as permission to "stain" this moment. Conversely, the ego always seeks to hold everyone else, including us, as a prisoner to the past mistakes that were made. I realized that for both Kate and Dale, a deeper look at future/fear and past/guilt associations was necessary for them to take the next step in their healing. I knew from my experience and through assisting others who had traveled down the infidelity path that time could be used to either heal or wound, but that the ego preferred it to be used as a double-edged sword made up of fear and guilt. For the ego, the fear edge was effective in upholding a protective and defensive posture, while the guilt edge was of equal value because of its effectual use to issue shame and paralysis. I wanted to eliminate both. For this couple, freedom and new beginnings were only going to be achievable by living in the moment.

I asked Dale how he was doing and he replied that things were not going well for him. He was beginning to go from the fear of losing his wife to anger. This transition was predictable, since the experience of betrayal and infidelity so closely parallels what we feel when we experience a death. Dale shared that he was spending much of his day going over everything, and he was imagining Kate and their neighbor, Phil, having sex. He was angry with them, and he was considering telling Phil's wife.

I explained to Dale that revenge is a desire of the ego, and it was always based upon the belief that the past is still happening *now*. Revenge was desired by his ego because it believed that to hurt another in the way it had been hurt would mitigate its pain. Then I reminded him that this was the illusion, and reviewed that what is shared is increased by its sharing. Consequently, if he created more pain, then he would distance himself from his goal of peace and love. I helped him to understand that he was allowing the past (guilt) mistake to stain the now, spawning a certain future hellish experience. I asked Kate to tell the story *for the very last time*.

Kate sat silenced, and was clearly afraid of the suggestion. I asked Dale if Kate's repeating the story would help him heal. He said it would help him to feel vindicated. I asked him if it was his heart or his head that wanted to make the call. He replied that it was his head. Then I asked him if he still wanted to repair the marriage. "Of course," he answered. I said that then, although it was normal to want to go over the "story" again and again, he would have to let it go after this last recall. Kate shared the details again. I asked him if there was anything left that was still misunderstood. He said no, then burst out with a haunting question to Kate: "Was he better in bed than me?" Kate took a deep breath and said, "No, not really." "Not really?" he replied. "What is that supposed to mean?" "Well," she answered, "he did always take care of my needs and you didn't, but then Phil is also not as cuddly as you are, so it is a trade-off."

Knowing that this discussion could just stimulate more hurt for both parties, I changed the subject. I asked Dale if he understood the deepest meaning of forgiveness, and to whom it should be offered in this situation. He said that he thought he did. Forgiveness would be offered to Kate, and he was not sure if he could give it totally. I nodded, and shared what I understood forgiveness to mean. I explained the foundation upon which forgiveness, in fact, becomes unnecessary.

Forgiveness usually means that I forgive you for doing something unloving to me. In short, I am willing to get over the transgression. This seems kind at first, but it is not. The truth is that we are not at the effect of fear or the ego unless we *want to be*. And the ego does want guilt and blame, but our spirit does not. The reality is that whatever was unloving came from the ego and *in truth* cannot affect me, unless I (my ego) decide I want it to. If I want the mistake to hurt me, I will allow it so that I can be "better than" my transgressor, rather than equal to them. If I decide to allow the fear-based, unloving action to affect me, then I have made the other party guilty and in need of *my* forgiveness. However, if I realize that the transgressor's ego cannot affect me, no forgiveness is needed. And in my decision to be only at the effect of the other's *spirit*, both of us are freed from guilt and blame. They are freed from the mistake they made, and I am freed from wanting them to feel guilt for hurting me.

Fidelity and Love

Our Creator is and has always been completely faithful to us, as we have been faithful to our Creator, but if we do not accept this to be true, we will maintain an ancient memory of the belief that we both betrayed and were betrayed by love (God). The separation from love or, biblically speaking, the departure from the Garden of Eden, really never occurred; rather, fear blocked our experience of omnipresent love, which we experienced in and as *the garden*, from which we were extended and within which we still are. Our "blindness" to this fact, and the restoration of awareness to love's constant presence, is what defines forgiveness.

This process of restoring our awareness to the truth facilitates experiences that move us up the ladder from specialness to human love, and finally to soulful love. However, since we wished to experience something other than perfection and thus "forgot" our real self, which in turn initiated the desire for something other than love (the desire for specialness), we thought we were unfaithful to love. I believe that, consequently, our great need for fidelity now also stems from this pain-filled memory of betrayal that we think we accomplished through the belief in separation. In having faithful relationships with one another, we can avoid stirring up the ancient wound that resides in our memories. Further, through the enforcement of fidelity, we hoped to avoid the painful sting of betrayal's memory, because we did not know we could explore whether betrayal was even possible.

In not examining the false belief in betrayal, and in recognizing that love is always committed to itself, the ego uses the belief in betrayal as yet another way to sustain itself. The ego issues the idea that we betrayed love (God) as a way to keep us running away from our source. Now let's consider the arrogance in the belief that we could actually be guilty, when we were created innocent. We need to be reminded that we may be able to block love like we can block light with the raising of our hand, but blocking should not be confused with obliterating. The ego uses our belief in our being a betrayer of love to sustain itself and become the "savior" that would protect us from our certain annihilation for such a "sin".[6] Consequently, we turn to the ego and the special relationship to mitigate any "due" punishment that we have been hypnotized into believing our Creator would lay upon us.

In our desire for autonomy and the special relationship, we, for the first time, experienced betrayal. However, the real betrayal is not the betrayal of God, but rather it is the betrayal of our own idea of self.

I asked Kate if she could forgive herself for the acts of infidelity she had engaged in. Kate replied that she was trying to. I told her that her hunger for intimacy, her ego identification, and fear were what really required forgiveness (undoing). I asked her to separate, in her mind, her real self from her ego identification. She did so, and relief rather than pain filled her face. I asked Dale to do the same. I explained to both of them that had they held on to their authentic self-identification, neither would have betrayed the other nor themselves, since betrayal is an ego-orientated idea, which has as its goal the sustaining of guilt. I shared that forgiveness was the

---

[6] The word "sin" is defined in the Course as nothing more than a term meaning "lack of love." To sin means to believe that there could be a lack of love, which the Course teaches cannot really be true; we can only delude ourselves into that belief.

undoing of the belief that either of them were egos. I suggested that compassion rather than guilt was the salve which they both thirsted for. I reminded Dale that he and Kate had lost sight of themselves as abundant, loving beings, and so they had acted out of their egos' insatiable hunger that can never be quenched without attacking the other person. They both sat silent, and it was clear that they had not previously shone the idea of infidelity through this lens of understanding.

I asked them to return with letters of self-forgiveness—in other words, letters of undoing what they believed they had done while under the influence of *fear*, describing experiences they were hiding and over which they were filled with shame that they now knew could be *erased through the love in this moment* rather than being maintained through past guilt and future fear. I said we would share their letters at the next meeting.

Our Greater Self

I am often asked to give an analogy of how we can simultaneously experience being an individual and a collective being, and how it came to pass that we lost our memory of being both. The following is offered as such an analogy:

Through the eternal and inseparable relationship of Cause (God) and Effect, the child of God—collectively represented in each entity—validates the other's existence. The awe-inspiring dance of inter-dependence and equality between the lover and the beloved becomes illuminated. Since each being is established by the other's presence, the relationship is interdependent and inseparable in nature.

I liken this "dance" to the one that happens through manifesting more "selves" when we are standing in front of a multi-paneled mirror. Notice how the first image or self that the mirror reflects is the image or self that determines the appearance of each subsequent image. Add more mirrors, and even more selves emerge—all without a cost to any of the prior images—and each of them as perfect as all the rest. In fact, the more mirrors there are, the more selves happen. What if each of those selves could be animated by breathing life into it and given free will or free thought to go and explore their greatness and fullness eternally? Then what if some of those selves did not like certain parts of themselves and began to hide them by wearing masks and coverings? What if then they began to clothe themselves to be unique and special? Soon they would forget what they originated from, and thus would need some other "mirror image" to remind them how to love the covered and unloved parts. What if then, as they accomplished that act of self-loving and appreciation, they began to undress and remember who they are? And what if, through their remembering, they finally began loving all the "images" as a part of themselves? From this analogy, we can deduce that love-based relationships are interdependent in nature, allowing an individualized experience, yet not diminishing the completeness of each being. With the awareness of our completeness, we are compelled by the dynamics of our authentic nature to share this abundance. Our real self offers all that it is and has, not only with its mate, but with all of humanity.

Further, since each real self-identity feels full and complete, they are not looking for anything or anyone outside of themselves to make them feel more valued or loved. Lastly, when an individual knows who they are, they are no longer searching for another soul in order to feel lovable themselves. Instead, they want to share their completeness and loveliness with a mate as an expression of what they are, just as the Creator did with us.

As parents, we can love and be in committed and intimate relationships with two or more children without a cost to either one of them, and I do believe we will some day mature enough to do the same with whomever we are drawn towards to share our fullness and unbounded love.

Until such a time arrives when we can love this completely, I believe that being monogamous is necessary to help us overcome our fear of intimacy and transparency. In consciousness and in our deeper awareness of what love is, I believe that the collective "we" is still in an adolescent stage. And just as we place parameters around our teenagers because they have not yet matured sufficiently to understand the full impact of each of their decisions, so, too, is the fidelity model helpful to assist us in the maturation process of the macro-self that we have forgotten.

The True Purpose of the Body

In the Course, we are taught that there is a tendency for us, in our ego-orientation, to over-emphasize the importance and value of the body. The body is said to be the result of desiring and upholding guilt. I think this is particularly true when broaching the subject of fidelity. The idea of being in several fully expressive (mind, body, and soul), intimate, love-honoring relationships simultaneously threatens our ego-orientation of what love is.

For many, the body is seen as sacred—powerful, important, and useful. We identify with the body, and so we go to great lengths to feed, clothe, adorn, and protect it. The mind and its power, on the other hand, are often minimized. The concept that mind is one and shared by all is often either denied or cringed at. We are not so eager to see our minds exposed. Yet, this is our true nature. The soul, too, is growing through its many ongoing relationships. So, it is only the body that is so revered as sacred that it should be coveted by, and shared with, only our mate.

The Course teaches that the body is neutral, and that it is a learning device for the mind. It states that love (God) did not create the body, because we were created perfectly as spirit. The body was created out of our desire to be something other than spirit. Since a remaking of self is impossible, we could only dream up a new self. The body is the manifested form of the wish to be different. The body has no abilities of itself, only the mind does, and the body expresses the mind's wishes and delusions. Further, the mind is what animates every cell of the body, and that is why the body is such a powerful learning tool for the mind. The body is to be used as a communication device, but we are taught that, in time, it will become unnecessary because we will eventually return to our natural form of communication, using only the mind.

Since we identify so strongly with the body, it is no wonder that we want to protect it so dearly. In fact, we feel justified in punishing others if they hurt another person's body, while we look the other way when someone says something that is aimed to hurt their soul. We have a global belief system that allows us to protect the body far more than love and innocence.

When an individual has made the decision to give the gift of fidelity, it is often for one of two reasons. First, it could be because they have a moral or religious belief system that they are consciously or unconsciously upholding. Second, it could be because they have come to realize that they are not sufficiently evolved to create intimacy without exclusivity. They hope that through the dance of intimacy that is nurtured by their relationship dynamics, they will arrive at a place where fear has been eradicated and perfect love is all that remains. For such a soul, this work can best be accomplished when they are not simultaneously engaged in other sexual relationships, as Kate discovered.

Dale and Kate returned to my office with letters of self-forgiveness in hand. Each openly shared their realizations, and they listened passionately to the other's secrets of their respective mistakes of the past. Dale spoke about his discovery of how afraid he was of not being good enough. Of things he had done that were dishonest and unkind, revealing lies he had told both Kate and others. He shared how controlling and afraid he was, and how cruel and intimidating he had been. Kate shared how she had cherished being victimized, had spied on Dale, and how she discovered that she had unconsciously started the affair so that she could cause the marriage to either change or end. Healing was clearly underway, for both. I decided it was time to discuss the body and its often overemphasized importance, and the minimization of the significance of the soul. I wanted to move Dale and Kate from special love relationship dynamics into human love, understanding, and compassion.

Dale and Kate discussed their respective desires to feel wanted and loved, and they both admitted that they had each had a great deal of hunger that had been left unsatisfied. Dale also made it clear that he wanted and expected monogamy in his relationship. Kate agreed. Kate then challenged Dale with respect to some suspicious activities he had engaged in with a woman from his office in previous years. Kate told him that she thought he had crossed the fidelity boundary with that woman. Dale knew exactly whom Kate was referring to, but denied any sexual activity. Kate then asked if he had cheated emotionally. Dale looked puzzled.

I explained to Dale that for some, an emotional affair was as crippling as a physical affair was on the marriage, and possibly even more so. I reminded him that whether one or the other hurt someone more was dependent upon that person's values. Some cherished the body as sacred, and some the heart. Dale was exposed, and in that moment, it became clear to the three of us that he had done to Kate emotionally what she had done to him physically. I suggested to them that they had each filled their hungers outside the marital union, and that the future success of their relationship depended on each partner's asking for what they respectively needed or wanted to feel appreciated and valued.

Dale and Kate worked with me intensively for two more months, and each of them learned that to keep their marriage growing, they needed to grow individually as well. They agreed not to talk about the events of either affair anymore, and to rather live in the moment. Dale learned that he was indeed accountable for the frailty of his marriage and continues to work at listening and caring for Kate and her needs. Kate has learned to speak up when things feel wrong or she is feeling oppressed. She has embraced her accountability for being too passive, noncommunicative, and acting like a doormat in order to feel spiritually superior. They have survived the infidelity and have a much better relationship than they once did. In fact, they are now flirting with the dance of soulful love.

As has been illuminated, most of us have a need to feel attractive and wanted, and when that is not how we feel, we seek out someone who will help us to feel that way. Until we truly know and cherish our sense of self-worth, we will be prey to the ego's insatiable hunger to be fed by the belief that we are valueless, and in lack. And when we awaken to the reality that each person is a gift in that they "mirror" what we believe about ourselves, or treat us as we believe ourselves to be worthy of being treated, we will become liberated in a very real sense.

By using the mirroring "barometer," I can remain aware of what my unconscious beliefs about myself are. And if I adore and cherish myself, so *must my partner*. And when we take personal responsibility for our contribution to the reactions and behaviors we receive from the people in our lives, we demonstrate adulthood and our power to change these behaviors.

Lastly, until our ache to finally feel good enough is soothed by the truth and acceptance of our identity and inheritance, infidelity in some form seems unavoidable. Once again, I have deduced that love is faithful to itself, and it is unassailable by any ego or micro-self action or inaction.

If you have been touched by infidelity, you have been given a bittersweet gift that is intended to test the understanding and depth of your love, or the lack thereof. Infidelity itself is not the real wound, but the abolishment of faith and trust in another human is. The pain we feel in our being at such a time is the heart-sent signal alarming us to the awareness that the *choice* to close our heart to the other person will not heal the wound, but that love will. The act of infidelity is always spawned by a search for self-love, and the healing is the supplying of it. Infidelity's sting is soothed by the absolute willingness to allow the love that had been blocked, to flow freely and abundantly.

Chapter Nine

Inseparable Energies—
A Sacred Dance

If we are truly going to embrace the new marriage paradigm, we must learn about the fullest expression of our feminine and masculine powers. Further, we must come to appreciate similarities and differences of each side, and their respective strengths and weaknesses. Now let's explore how each side contributes to the sacredness of the marriage union.

In order to fully participate in the deepest level of intimacy with another person, we must first know and appreciate ourselves. And if we ever hope to become fully conscious and aware of our total makeup and access the power that is imbedded within us, we must own and embrace our feminine and masculine sides—our shadow and light sides. As we explore our deeper nature, we will awaken to the fact that, at a core level, the feminine and masculine energies are present within us in equal proportions. Further, although both energies are equally present, one side will be magnified, and our gender is reflective of which side we are "majoring" in.

With this awareness in mind, let's imagine that we are a magnet. As magnets, we would recognize that in order to express our full "nature"—our two sides—we would need to do two things: repel and attract. The repelling side pushes things outward; it is the energy that makes things manifest. To state it differently, we could say that the feminine is the idea, while the masculine is the expression or manifestation of the idea. Neither could be experienced without the other—these forces are inseparable. And each side proves that the other exists. The feminine side (idea or seed) allows itself to be fertilized into a new form. The union of both energy forces manifests a nurturing womb that allows things to grow into their fullest expression.

The spirit, which is a fast-moving vibration of light, is most often invisible to the eyes, yet it is the animating force behind the grosser, or denser and slower-moving expression of light that we call matter.

In the earth-plane, we manifest as either male or female, so that we can experience and grow through that gender's power and weakness. Since both masculine and feminine forces are equally within our total makeup, and our gender is a symbol of the side we are "magnifying," it is critical to appreciate both sides. The soul chooses through which side it will manifest—the feminine or the masculine. The decision is made because one of the two sides is evaluated to have the greatest potential to facilitate the process of awakening us to our fullest expression of love (God). God, or the Great Orchestrating Design, is a perfect balance of both energies, and so are we in our authentic nature. Ultimately, if we are to know ourselves, we will simultaneously reveal our Creator—the Mother/Father energies that are God.

An emotionally, psychologically, mentally, and spiritually matured man or woman, who is capable of embracing the fullest expression of the power their gender offers, does not seek for power or control, because they *know* they have both. They are no longer searching for these qualities because they have outgrown the need to compete against the opposite sex to establish their worth and abilities. They have come to love and appreciate the differences between the sexes.

A new era began for women in 1920, when they were first permitted to vote. Westernized women are still seeking for equality in pay and responsibilities in the workforce. This hunger is the direct result of the oppression of women in the twentieth century. Women who have been feeling less valued by men have the urge to compete against them to prove their abilities and worth. The fact that they felt less worthy as women has stunted their emotional maturing. The emotionally young female presents in the world as highly competitive, hard, and cold, but in truth, she is just terrified of her unconscious feminine feelings of inadequacy, helplessness, and powerlessness—feelings that both men and women have and struggle to become comfortable with.

On the flip side, an emotionally matured woman knows and appreciates her abilities and weaknesses, and is able to access both her masculine and feminine creative energies as a result. She respects the differences that both energies envelop, and values them equally. The emotionally mature feminine does not use her nature to overpower or control anyone;

instead she surrenders and welcomes her strong receptive feminine self as her power, much like an ocean, which, being situated at a lower level than rivers and streams, allows all other waters to flow into it. The rivers and streams feed and fill the ocean.

The Power of Surrender

The shadow side of the feminine position arises in any moment that she cannot embrace her need to receive. The traits that then surface are control, seductiveness, and domination—she exudes these qualities to gain or hold power. A woman who has learned the powerfully healing and transformative process of surrendering will feel that to do so is both natural and powerful, and will not view her surrender as a submissive posture. The man she is with will intuitively then lift her *above* himself and glorify her beauty and power. This is the sacred "dance" of balance, equality, and respect that will birth a more soulful love.

To arrive at a place where we, as women, are in stable positions of power through being nurturing, softer, gentler, and surrendered to the strong, protective male in our life is a process that we undergo through the power struggles within the relationship. This process can sometimes be messy and even violent, and it will often unveil deep, unconscious feelings of fear because we are all so terrified of being viewed as vulnerable and powerless.

The fear of surrendering to one another in a relationship is indicative of our deeper fear of love, intimacy (transparency), and not being good enough, or safe. And to the degree that we feel powerless, in danger (real or imagined), and afraid inside, we will be striving to avoid these feelings by controlling each other and our outside world of experience.

Balancing Head and Heart

To understand more fully the incredible force that fear holds over our behaviors, let's look at the workings of the brain. Dr Paul MacLean, a neurologist, holds a theory known as the Triune Brain, in which he categorizes the brain into three levels: the neocortex, the *thinking brain*; the limbic system, the *emotional brain*; and the basal ganglia, the *survival brain*. Each part is interrelated, yet each has its own patterns and needs. In the book *Passage to Intimacy* by Lori H. Gordon, PhD (Fireside, 2001), there is a brief summary of each, which I will explain further.

The *survival brain* is preoccupied with issues of survival, safety, and territory. It craves order, routine, and regularity, and if these "patterns" are threatened, it will become insistent that we find them. This is the memory-storing part of the brain, which can recall potentially dangerous experiences that have touched the individual's personal and the collective human history. It is from this place within us that the self-preservation drive originates. There are two basic survival questions that this part of the brain issues: "Is it safe? Will I survive?" This part of the brain is largely masculine in energy.

The *emotional brain* fosters deep feelings of nurture and bonding, which help us in successfully raising our young and protecting our family group. This is the region that fosters humor, playfulness, and the desires of the inner child. It also houses our deeper feelings of love, joy, grief, and hate, and searches for emotional survival and the desire to procreate. This brain region holds emotional memories and is stimulated by sound and by sound-fostered communication. The basic question this region asks is, "Is it pleasurable or painful?" This region is largely feminine in energy.

The neocortex is the intellectual, thinking, cognitive part of the brain. It is the "womb" of ideas and inventions. This region asks us to consider if things are reasonable or logical. The senses—the eyes, ears, and our sense of touch—stimulate the thinking brain. This region searches for material objects: cars, houses, tools, things not human; it is heartless and cold and functions more like a computer than a feeling human.

Information that reaches the *thinking brain* is first passed through the *emotional brain*, where it becomes "colored" and is assessed as to how much attention should be paid to it. In short, emotional needs and assumptions deeply affect our thinking and behavior; in fact, our emotions can "hijack" our abilities to reason things out. The *thinking brain* is largely masculine in energy.

As we explore the different levels of the brain and what each region is interested in doing, we can also discover why we struggle so much with the opposite sex. Suddenly, the idea of women coming from Venus and men coming from Mars becomes very clear. The masculine part of us is interested in the intellect and in the three "p's": providing, protecting, and procreating. It is interested in what makes logical sense; it explores and defines that which is reasonable, while the feminine part of us is emotionally driven.

To the same degree that women have been struggling to find their power and place in the corporate and business world, men have been struggling to make sense of the home front. In the switching of roles, both sexes have been called to develop the less prominent parts of their fullest natures. In the world of business and career advancement, setting feelings aside and using the *thinking brain* and its capacity to reason and use the intellect to gather resources and find answers to problems is a necessity. In fact, those abilities do facilitate financial and business success, and it is equally true that these facilities also become the crippling agents to the development of the close emotionally intimate relationship we crave to have with our mate.

Men can and do help women with the power of discernment and with using their intellect to reason and rationalize their strong emotional pull. And it is equally true that women can help a man get in touch and be comfortable with his feeling side. The goal for each sex is to balance head and heart.

Now let's begin to explore how men and women mature into their masculine/feminine energies differently. Little girls are expected to express emotions, and they are much more likely to be appreciated for their strong feelings and emotional expressions. Boys, on the other hand, are often advised to suppress their feelings from a very young age. They are told to "chin-up," "cowboy-up," or be "big boys" and are instructed that big boys do not cry.

In his book *Why Marriages Succeed or Fail: And How You Can Make Yours Last* (Simon & Schuster, 1995), John Gottman, PhD, brings to light some poignant facts about the natural differences between the sexes: "The first problem for future marriages arises in preschool, when boys and girls begin to play separately. You can often hear little boys on the playground taunting girls, 'Go away. This is a *boys' game*. We hate girls.' And girls—even when they are building with blocks rather than playing house—want to get rid of the boys. 'Leave us alone. Boys are gross.'"

Later in his book, Gottman shares statistics that show how we begin sex segregation as we age. 36 percent of preschool children say they have friends of the opposite sex, but by the time they reach kindergarten, only 23 percent do. By the time children are in grade four or five, we almost never see mixed gender groups working or playing together unless they were instructed to do so.

"Because of this preference, boys and girls grow up in parallel universes where most of the emotional rules are different," says Gottman. "This may be where the trouble between the sexes begins."

Boys tend to be louder, more aggressive, and love to do rough-and-tumble play. Girls like to play more quietly, closer to the school building, and in smaller groups. Boys play on a team to compete against each other or some other team, and feel bonded by team effort. Boys overlook emotions to keep the "ball in play," while girls will quit if someone gets hurt. Girls play games and role-play to feel emotionally connected to one another, while boys play to feel connected to themselves.

By age ten, little boys have received the message from their peers, and unfortunately often also from their parents, that to show their emotions is terribly un-cool or un-manly! They learn to hide feelings behind a mask of toughness or indifference. In fact, if a boy gets hurt on the playing field, you will see him grimace as he squeezes his face, bites his lip, and hides his face if he cannot hold back a tear or two. A girl, on the other hand, will take a hit, then voice her pain, crunch into a ball, and cry out her tears as nearly everyone will show her their concern and, if at all possible, stop the activity or game to attend to her "pain." With these key differences in our reactions to each gender, is it any wonder, then, that couples struggle so much with the expression and receiving of each other's feelings?

In his book, Gottman also brings to light the biological differences in men and women in the sense that men are far less able to sustain a normal heart rate when they discuss emotionally charged topics. Men become "flooded with adrenaline, and they become overwhelmed by the strong feelings that are emitted by the *emotional brain*. Typically, they will then 'shut down' and 'stonewall' their mate. They recluse into their 'cave' as a way of coping with the ocean of feelings that they have within them but have been conditioned to hide rather than express."

Another interesting biological difference between the sexes can be found in the arena of our "X" and "Y" chromosomes. In his article *Even Neanderthals Get the Blues*, published in the June 2005 issue of *O, The*

Oprah Magazine, Russel Banks discusses how men think, feel, and process the world differently than women. The facts explained in this article allowed me to unveil yet another piece in the puzzle of why the genders react so differently to the experience of life. For instance, many men tend to be "conquerors." Let's look at a possible reason why this is so.

According to Banks' article, "it's long been known that of their three billion DNA units, human beings and their nearest relatives, chimpanzees, share 98.5 percent of the same genomes. That's awfully close. Genetically speaking, there is a greater difference between the eastern and western Bluebird. It's also long been known that both the male human and the male chimpanzee carry a Y chromosome. Recently, thanks to research including the Human Genome Project, we've learned that there are 78 genes attached to that male's Y chromosome that are not possessed by the female of either species. What this means if we're talking chromosomes is that a male human being is closer to a male chimpanzee than he is to a female human being."

I have concluded that men are biologically "hardwired" and constructed to do three primary things to ensure both sexes' physical survival: the masculine force is on purpose and fulfilled when it procreates, provides, and protects. Consequently, when the masculine part of our nature, or a man, fulfills these tasks, he feels accomplished, in control, and powerful, and if the female complains about some unmet emotional need, men feel confused and powerless, and will, generally, run or withdraw into their "cave."

Remember, we are all both masculine (thinkers) and feminine (feelers), and at all times, and in different situations, will act in accordance with either the thinking or the feeling part of our nature. As a woman, I at times want to conquer, protect, provide, and procreate just as does a man. However, my preference or default reaction is to feel my way through situations and experiences, rather than just intellectualize them. Men spend the majority of their time expressing through the masculine (the repelling side of the energy magnet), just as women spend their primary time experiencing life through the feminine (the attracting side of the energy magnet). Maturity of the total being occurs as a result of enveloping both the masculine and feminine facets. This is accomplished when we can appreciate and balance the two complimentary forces.

Talking with Allan about how he processes the world in general has facilitated in me a greater compassion and appreciation for the masculine force. It has also verified for me that Allan is *predominantly* driven to do three things: protect, provide, procreate—or rather, engage in procreative activities!

From his answers to my many questions about how he runs his trucking dealerships, I learned a lot about what he felt was most natural for him to do. His duties include managing people, resolving staff conflicts, strategizing future industry growth, handling truckers' complaints, drafting business plans, negotiating large truck orders, designing building expansions and improvements, dealing with contractors, reviewing budgets, and tracking inventory. He discloses candidly that for him, the emotionally charged duties, such as dealing with staff conflicts, are the most unnerving, yet most rewarding emotionally. It feels most foreign to his masculine makeup to do "feelings work."

In Allan's opinion, his female controller is much better equipped to handle the more emotional issues with the female staff, because she is a woman and can deal with the strong emotions that women are more conditioned to express. Allan has also come to realize that he can mature emotionally through working with the males within the organization. It seems logical that he understands them better than his controller because he is a man. What Allan admits to having learned is that allowing and even inviting the strong and loud expressions of feelings of anger, hate, and rage between the conflicted parties can be critical to the eventual resolution. Rather than minimizing or placating the verbal expressions of frustration, he creates a safe space to have his unhappy, frustrated staff and management "let it all out."

I shared with Allan how, in my counseling work, I invite emotionally wounded couples to "move" their anger in the presence of their partner by using sounds and movements instead of words. Once they've done this, they are able to talk about their upsets without attacking the other person—their feelings of anger no longer distort their words. Allan felt uncomfortable using the "sounds-and-movements-only" approach, so, in his business, he tried a modified version of the exercise and found it to be effective for his needs. When he works with the staff at his dealership, he lets them say whatever they want, provided it is about the behaviors of the other person and not about them personally.

In addition to being effective with couples, this process appears to work well between males, although I have found it is not as effective when it is done between two women. Women tend to hold on to words and internalize them and shut down. For women, words can feel more like punches than expressions or symbols of upset. Allan has experienced repeatedly that when men can just say what they have been repressing, they eventually calm down and find their own solutions for creating a better relationship. This is so because when people feel weak, they become defensive and self-absorbed, and lose the ability to listen. When they are given space and time to voice their hurts and frustrations, they move from being self-absorbed (the basal ganglia or the survival part of the brain) to responsiveness (the neocortex or thinking brain), which means they begin to shift and have the capacity to hear another person's view. In this movement, there is a shift from a conversation that is degenerative and dehumanizing to a constructive one in which resolutions can be offered up to support one another.

I believe that all people regardless of gender have a basic need to be heard and received by the person to whom they are expressing. When we can create a platform for a conflicted party to speak, be received, and then ask the listener to reflect back what they heard from the speaker, without defending against what was shared, conversation moves from weak, self-absorbed, and deaf, to recognition, strength, and mutual empowerment. Allan has been able to confirm this theory primarily through working with the men in his organization. As a result, he is beginning to welcome, rather than resist, the natural conflicts that arise when people have to work together.

While Allan admits that he enjoys the hands-on "mental mechanics" of running his operation, he also confesses that he finds the "head stuff" to be easier in his role as a stepfather. For him, nurture is given by tossing the football, watching sports together, looking under the hood of the kids' vehicles, providing funds for post-secondary education, and teaching them how to repair almost anything. He does admit, however, that he hungers for more heart-to-heart interaction.

Through my conversations with Allan about the differences between men and women, as well as through working with clients, I have come to appreciate that the masculine side prefers to figure out things, rather than figure out feelings.

I know with certainty that I yearn for more emotional closeness with Allan, even though that yearning terrifies him because he is not sure how to fulfill my desire. I can make great strides in achieving greater emotional closeness with him by doing just a couple of things. I can tell him that he is right when we see or feel differently about an experience or an event that we have shared in. I have learned that my willingness to surrender my need to be right makes him more receptive to my point of view or to the request I am making. I can also tell him that although he is right, I could use some help in feeling heard and understood. Remember that men tend to be conquerors first, so by letting him feel that he is in power, I get what I need. Lastly, I can do something very magical for him and us: I can let him know he is *already* the greatest man in the world *for me*, which will make him feel received and deeply wanted.

Now, let's look at the evolutionary process that men and women undergo as we learn about the inseparable forces of the feminine and masculine within us.

Maturing through the Feminine

I remember observing my mother as a young girl, and I can still recall thinking, "When girls grow into women, their power changes." Years later, I found this to be true. What occurs is that we (men and women) mature in our ability to gracefully embrace feminine power.

This evolutionary process is usually undertaken as a result of uncovering suppressed emotions. However, since we have somewhat programmed men and young boys into believing that to show feelings is "bad" and unmasculine, weak, and unattractive, we have created a stumbling block for both men and women to stride over in order to deepen intimacy between the couple. We want a more feeling man, yet we pursue the "bad boy" character.

Many women are attracted to the "bad boy" personality—the guy who enforces his will through a rough-and-tough persona like that so often portrayed by Clint Eastwood in his roles on the "big screen." Women are at times very attracted to a man who will direct "his woman" to do what she is told—to surrender to his will. In part, we desire this interaction with the persona of the "bad boy" behavior because we intuitively know that the animating feminine force, or spirit, does surrender to the masculine, which expresses as physical matter.

This surrender does not occur as an act of submission or an expression of inequality or an imbalance of power, but rather it occurs by necessity in order to have physical expression of any form. In part, we want a man to find and share his feelings and in part, we do not. We also want men to be tough protectors. Men are often mystified and terrified by these mixed desires. Many men simply feel that the work of exploring and sharing feelings is a "girl," or feminine, thing to do, and they are correct.

In truth, however, a man cannot reach his full masculine potential without maturing his feminine energies. The reciprocal is true for women. A woman cannot mature into her fullness until she has matured her masculine, particularly until she learns not to allow her emotional brain to rule her ability to reason. Further, even women need to grow in their maturity and in the ability to express their feelings in an uncontaminated way. Women tend to be passive-aggressive in their verbalizations until they grow in emotional maturity.

Men who have emotionally not grown into adulthood will find the feminine force as frightening as do many emotionally immature women. A man who is not comfortable with the inevitable feelings of powerlessness (surrender) that envelop the feminine will move quickly to a defensive posture or total denial of the feelings that are aroused by interacting with the feminine (feelings) part of their being. Men will traditionally use vocalizations to override the deep feelings that make them feel out of control.

Men and women struggle equally when they are not in a position of control, because they associate powerlessness with weakness instead of with strength. Powerlessness and surrender are expressions of strength because they do not use energy to defend against. They eradicate fear, and they are synonymous with love because they allow, accept, and appreciate what is.

The degree to which we can mature into our brilliance as masculine/feminine beings is in direct proportion to our ability to love, respect, see, and be seen and appreciated by, our mothers and fathers, regardless of whether they are on earth or have crossed over into the world of spirit. This healing is imperative to the maturing of the respective energy forces because our parents are our models of the male and female within us. In essence, they are the physical expressions of the masculine and feminine God (love). Love in the feminine is the being, and in the masculine, it is love's expression or extension. Again, each becomes known through the other.

As girls, we tend to model after our mothers, and we are called to mature into our womanhood and learn to embrace and become responsible for the awesome feminine power that moves through us. The emotional child within us is encouraged to grow from infancy to adulthood. The growth occurs through close examining of many beliefs that we had adopted and formulated early in our lives, and which we need to update. We adopted these beliefs, perceptions, and notions to protect us from any future pain. The outdated reactions become our present-day defenses. The child in us does not want to be hurt, abandoned, or rejected, but most of all, the child is terrified of being wrong!

When the emotional child has sufficiently matured, this process of maturation is then furthered through a careful sorting and understanding of the painful experiences we feel we have had with men. Many of us had the first painful experience with the masculine when we were little girls. We may have had an experience that left us feeling overpowered, rejected, inadequate, invisible, or unsafe with our fathers, who represented the face of the masculine.

Many of the experiences and patterns that we repeatedly encounter in our adult life were formed early on. Over the years, we have created elaborate defensive structures to keep us safe and to hide our desperate search for power.

Through an ongoing and honest reflection of self, and through owning and appreciating both the light and dark sides of our full feminine nature, we evolve. We embark upon an emotionally maturing journey from toddler to child into adolescence, and then on to young adulthood. Finally, one magical day, we awaken to the fact that we have matured into our adulthood—the wise woman.

The miraculous process of maturing our capacity to envelop the full feminine in turn matures our man's ability to do the same, and it will ultimately evolve the marriage. In short, the marriage is as mature as the people in it. As each soul matures in both the feminine and masculine, so, too, does the marriage transit from young through adolescence, and then into grown adult.

I believe that for many of us, this journey takes a full lifetime—if we are consciously working on intimacy and maturing the self. I also believe that for others among us, it may well take *several* lifetimes!

To embrace the feminine often means we must examine the archetype of mother. Regardless of whether they bore children, all women mother. For some, the mothering expresses in nurturing pets, and for others, it does so in the support of friends or colleagues. Mothering is an instinctual part of being a woman, and therefore looking at both the light and shadow sides of the mother's nature is important. There are many traits and qualities within the makeup of the mother that we have collectively polarized into two opposing sides—the positive, which we are proud to own or express, and the negative, which we wish to deny or disown. Some examples of qualities or traits are: possessive, nurturing, gentle, bitchy, domineering, compassionate, forgiving, and soothing.

The degree to which a woman has matured her emotional body by achieving balance with her *thinking brain* and has reclaimed her ability to listen to, receive, and hear her inner child's hurts, fears, and desires, is also the degree to which she has integrated the shadow side of her nature.

If we had a mother who was integrated emotionally and mentally, we are more likely to be emotionally "older" and less afraid of our feelings of powerlessness. If, on the other hand, we were raised by a mother with immature emotional skills, as I was, we will have a long journey to emotional (feminine) adulthood.

As we heal with our mother, which means that we have looked honestly at both the shadow and light sides of our mother and can own each part in ourselves, we mature. In being able to share who we are in our personalities and what makes us happy or sad, what inspires us, and what our deepest secrets are, and as we are able to disclose areas where we are both strong and weak, addicted, and afraid, we, and our mothers, heal and mature. Further, we can tell our moms what they have done to hurt and heal us. We can do so without blame or judgment. We can communicate our experience, and know that we have grown through both the support and the challenges that our mother and father presented.

I recommend that all couples who wish to grow in their marriage do this exercise with both parents. The inner child within us, and within our mate, is influencing us in our marriage, and we are continuously fostering experiences and issues that unearth the unresolved parental issues we hold. The marriage becomes the reenactment of the past, until we learn to love and appreciate our parents and our inner child.

When working with people who have deceased parents, I sit in as the surrogate. I just listen, receive, and share my gratitude for their transparent and honest communication. When I do so, they become free. The child that lives within them finally feels seen for all that they are—shadow and light, strong and weak, dependent and independent. And as we are able to be honest and grateful for our parental figures, we learn to speak without condemnation in our marital union.

Chapter Ten

Sacred Union

In this chapter, we will discuss the major stumbling blocks that often stand in the way of our manifesting a soulful, rather than special, relationship.

Our deepest level of growth is accomplished when we participate fully in our relationships. And the ultimate goal of our relationships is to awaken us to our divinity. Although relationships do not need to be romantic in nature to help us reach that goal, it is the romantic ones that can bring us to our knees, exposing our egos, our wounds, true emotional "age," and the most crippling illusions we hold, faster than anything else can.

It is natural for us to be in relationships, but it takes enormous courage and wisdom to embrace the dance of intimacy with another soul who has a "contract" that is designed to make us find, acknowledge, and appreciate our complete human nature.

Although we tend to categorize our traits and behaviors in either the shadow or light side of our makeup, the truth is that, above all of these defenses, we are simply love. I call all the behaviors and traits "defenses" because they are connected to our experience of being human, and all defenses are used to get "something": acceptance, attention, approval, autonomy, control, and power, and they issue from the part of the mind that feels separate and in need. The ego is the mask that represents the part of the mind (human) that is asleep and unconscious of its authentic Self (spirit).

Above the traits and defensive behaviors we engage in is a being that is only love, has only one feeling, which is joy, and whose sole experience is peace and contentment. The truth is, we are a being that is defenseless and recognizes itself to be unified with all other beings. It has no lack or need, so its only function is to extend its love and radiance.

If we consciously make the decision to do the intimacy "dance," we will expose and heal our fears, and through that journey, create a sacred and soulful relationship.

Inasmuch as we are aware of and can appreciate the similarities and key differences of the feminine and masculine forces, we foster the occurrence of miracles! Through appreciating these complimentary and inseparable forces, we are, as a couple, nurtured into fully being who we truly are. Each of the partners can facilitate the maturing of the dominant power in their mate—the feeling side or the intellect. Often it is men who need maturing in dealing with the feeling side of their nature, since they have generally been trained to use their intellect to succeed in the world of business. For women, growth comes from not allowing the feeling side to hijack reason and intellect, since they are more conditioned to do so. In some couples, however, the reverse is the case. Ultimately, we will have a balance between the head and heart, our intellect and feeling capabilities. And inasmuch as we make a commitment to be awakened and present to our authentic being, we are able to develop loving partnerships and are far less likely to engage in control dramas to secure power.

The merger of the maturing masculine and feminine energies creates a sacred union and facilitates an eternally soulful rather than temporal "special" relationship. A soulful relationship has many strong "stones" that can be cemented together to build a "house." These stones are trust, compassion, perseverance, tolerance, patience, honesty, understanding, openness, truthfulness, abundance, and equality. Therefore, a crucial step for the couple to take in transitioning their union from one of lack and specialness to one of abundance and soulfulness is to recommit *a more matured self* to one another.

An analogy that I use with couples in marriage coaching sessions to help illuminate the transition from a special relationship into a soulful one is the reconstruction of a house built from straw or wood to one built of stone. I explain that the old matrimonial "house" built of wood or straw had a specific goal, namely specialness (guilt, separation, and lack), while the new one built of stone will be driven by equality, abundance, and truth. Consequently, the stone house can withstand centuries of wear and tear—the exposing of all the cracked or immature emotional reactions.

The old straw or wood "house" was built by two emotionally young people, each searching for security and external power. This temporal "house" was designed to "shelter," rather than expose, the parts of themselves they were afraid of and didn't want to see.

Conversely, the new "home" is designed to expose the total self—shadow and light—healing the perceived lacks that each believed were there. In addition, I explain that it may well take a little longer to put each stone in place, but the structure itself will be able to withstand all emotional "climate and weather" challenges necessary to unveil each individual's divinity and authentic internal power. I remind the couple that our experience of the world (finance, health, family, social, mental, spiritual, and vocational aspects) is an external reflection of our inner beliefs, thoughts, and feelings of worthiness, and that therefore the reclaiming of our internal power is an absolute necessity if we want to see a different reality reflected. Since internal power is recognized proportionately to the degree to which we reclaim our authentic identity, our mate is indispensable in helping us achieve that goal. In short, what I believe about you is ultimately what I will believe about myself.

To build a stone house effectively, we need a very strong and stable foundation. The recommitment to the relationship serves as the mortar which holds the bricks and braces in place. Together, bricks, braces, and mortar make an even stronger marriage foundation—one that can hold up all the unending growth and expansion of the matrimonial "house." The new matrimonial "house," being both larger and deeper, fosters a greater capacity for its "occupants" to expand. As the souls grow, so does the house! This sacred "home" is designed to withstand the almost certain "emotional earthquakes" that arise when we become more self-aware. The arrival of these "quakes" is a sign that a much deeper and more conscious self-evaluation is underway.

Truthful Conversations

As we explored in detail in chapter seven, in order to create intimacy between the pair, there must be more truthful, self-exposing conversations. And as unnerving and ego-debilitating as it is to expose one's hidden thoughts and assumptions, it must be done if the couple desires a richer, more unconditional love to rule their union. Each person must be willing to talk about their feelings and emotions, including those that are most frightening. Each party must be willing to ask clearly for what they need, without judgment of it. They must recognize they are needy in some way, even if the need consists of being appreciated for who they are, or for their values, wants, and desires. Each will at times need to place parameters *around requests* the other makes of them, when they feel overwhelmed, afraid, or suffocated. And each must learn how to receive all of their mate's feelings and thoughts without condemnation. They will each need to learn how to listen and repeat back to their mate what it is that they heard, and in so doing, learn of the transformative power of being a witness.

The work of transparent conversations is deep, and my suggestion is that you find a qualified intimacy coach or a counselor trained in intimacy and marriage to help you get started.

Power and the Need to Be Right

In my belief, power struggles (arising from our incessant need to be right) are the most influential factor fostering the destruction of intimacy. Power struggles are at times necessary to reveal our fears, and may be useful to enhance closeness. However, this can be accomplished most effectively if we understand the differences between men and women and appreciate the benefits of the way each side processes information and experiences. As we mature, we no longer wish to change our mate, but rather use their different ideas and opinions as aids to facilitate mutual growth.

The reality is that power struggles emerge largely because we lose respect for our mate or no longer fully trust them with what is important to us. We think we know, more than they do, that our position is of more importance. Equality is the last thing on our minds when we are controlling someone. In the heat of a power struggle, our unconscious or our "inner child" begins to run the show, leading us to believe that we will lose something of more importance or value than our partner. This is true primarily because the ego does not value our partner as much as it cherishes being right. At some point, we need to value happiness more than being on top. When this decision *authentically* happens, we recognize that joy is ours each time we let the other person be right.

I make the point about authentically choosing happiness over being right because until we believe that making that choice is *not* a sacrifice to us, resentment rather than joy will surface. Each time you have the opportunity, ask yourself honestly if you want the joy of letting the other be right, or if you are just not ready *yet*. If you are truthfully still in need of being right or proving your position, go easy on yourself and take some time to reflect on the reasons why. Following your reflection, muster up the courage to discuss your fears around being wrong with your partner. Intimacy is sure to be the reward of such an endeavor! Be aware that all fear of allowing the other to be right comes from either our fear of facing our own feelings of inadequacy, or from a perceived loss of control, or equality. Lastly, the decision to allow others to be right demonstrates your wisdom and authentic power, while it minimizes or eliminates the other's defenses.

Receiving and Expressing Anger and Sadness

If we want to participate in a soulful union, we must have the wisdom and courage to completely receive one another, together with all the feelings we harbor, including rage. As a society, we are generally uncomfortable with witnessing expressions of anger and rage. From early on, our mothers and fathers told us that expressions of anger and, in the extreme, the temper tantrums we displayed, were unacceptable behaviors. This pattern of repressing our anger has been our guest through the millennia, as generation upon generation has adopted the belief that anger is bad, without examining if this is really true.

The problem inherent in such a belief is that as long as we categorize anger as bad, we will try to stuff it away, rather than channel it out constructively. If this fiery energy is repressed long enough, it will express in a passive-aggressive fashion or will eventually turn into a blowout of rage. Another fact worth considering is that what we *repress*, someone will *express*. This is true because of the law of energy dynamics—that every action has an equal and opposite reaction. Therefore, if three of four family members are repressing their anger, it is a safe bet that the one remaining person will be doing the expressing for the rest of the family!

Anger is a form of fear, and fear occurs in any moment that we are unaware of love's omnipresence. Fear (anger) is the belief that we are lacking love. Since we are fluctuating between love and fear all day, anger is harbored as well. Anger is an energy of clearing, much like fire is. It ignites and burns away our illusions. Anger that is expressed openly and honestly and is *not* directed at someone or something is transformative. When we learn to be with our own anger, we become much more equipped to hold others in their anger also. If we can be received, rather than corrected or rejected when we are engulfed in these powerful feelings, we feel deeply cared for, nourished, and loved. In fact, we feel *unconditionally* loved, which is the passageway to intimacy.

A healthy way to express anger is to make guttural sounds, which are much like the growls of an angry cat or lion. Another healthily channeled expression of anger is to punch pillows or a punching bag. I sometimes run to release my rage, or make primal sounds in my car when I feel the urge. Some people draw pictures, while others swing plastic bats. Since we have been discouraged since childhood from expressing our rage, it takes time until we become comfortable doing it. Begin by practicing alone, then try to have your intimate partner witness you while you release your anger. It is important to advise them that you are not "broken" or in need of consoling, but rather, that you are just moving your feeling of anger out of your mind and body. The desire to say, "I feel" tormented, rage, angry, upset, and so on, is fine. It is not appropriate to say, "*You* make me feel," although the ego will try to convince you that the other person is to blame for how you feel. We are ultimately responsible for creating our own feelings. In the beginning stages of using this technique, it is advisable to work with an experienced counselor who can help facilitate intimacy through this process.

When we are angry with our intimate partner, it is appropriate to share that we are feeling powerless, rejected, minimized, assaulted, afraid, patronized, and so on. Be aware that if we are being enveloped by any feelings other than joy and peace, it is because we have slipped back into "specialness" and are perceiving some form of lack. This process of fluctuating between our authentic and ego personas is expected, and through owning and admitting this fluctuation, we move through it. As each day passes, we will notice that we are spending more moments in our authentic identities and are less susceptible to the ego's defensive moves and opinions. The only way out of our anger is through it!

I believe that our inability to receive sadness from one another issues from our inability to receive our own feelings of sorrow. We have, as a society, been hypnotized not only into the belief that we should not express anger, but also into the idea that we should hide our pain. No emotion will ever leave our bodies by being repressed or ignored; it will only fester, until it becomes unmanageable. Further, the feelings will eventually express in hidden forms (mental and physical illness, stuttering, self-abusive behaviors, eating disorders, and depression) and be harder to identify. For instance, the uncontrollable urge to smoke cigarettes is driven by our need to run away from, and stuff down, our deeper feelings of sadness, powerlessness, and anger. The action of inhaling and holding smoke in our lungs, which are located in the heart region of the body, is indicative of our not wanting to face our more intense emotions. If you are not convinced of this connection, try it. Take a person (yourself or another) who smokes, and give them the support and encouragement to each day safely release their deep feelings of rage, powerlessness, and sadness, and within weeks or a few months of their emotional purging, they won't want to smoke any longer—I promise.

Sadness is an emotion that alerts us to the awareness that a wish or dream is not being realized, by ourselves or by someone else, and that it is time to share this and look for the fulfillment of the dream or wish in another form—one that is likely to be more difficult to identify.

Depression is internalized rage and unidentified, blocked sadness. Depression occurs when an individual has a fantasized notion that they, or their life, should be different—particularly that they or their life should not have a challenging side. The depression remains if a person refuses to acknowledge and allow all their emotions, traits, and characteristics to flow without passing judgment on them. If this affects your relationship, find a skilled therapist who can assist both parties in identifying and recognizing all their shattered wishes and dreams and the emotions surrounding that perceived loss.

For you as a partner in a soulful relationship, it is a requirement that you learn to receive your mate's sadness without needing to "fix" him or her. Your mate is not broken; it is a part of the human condition and growth process to be sad sometimes. The next time your spouse feels sad, just allow them to sit with their tears, hold them, and assure them that even in their sorrow, they are loved.

As we mature and own all of our feelings, including feelings of need, such as greed and possessiveness, they become integrated into our being, and we in turn are able to allow others to have and appreciate these same companions.

Destructive Inner Dialogues

As our relationship evolves from special to soulful, we will be in need of updating old beliefs. The beliefs that uphold the special relationship dynamics are, of course, always based on a belief in lack, incompetence, or autonomy. Consequently, we will need to search our minds for statements such as, "Here we go again, she is always…" or "He is never…" Other clues to search for are inner statements that bind our mate to who they were (months or years ago), instead of receiving them as who they have become. The ego compels us to live in the past, projecting the assumption that our mate is and will always be inadequate in some area. The idea that soul growth, emotional maturity, and some new, less defensive behaviors are being expressed is inconceivable to the ego, so it is quick to use inner statements that discount such growth. The following is an example:

Recently, I was working with a couple whose marriage was in crisis. The woman, whom I will call Jenny, was emotionally starving and consequently displayed behaviors that were congruent with such deprivation. When she spoke, she did so in a tone that was extremely defensive and aggressive. She was issuing numerous ultimatums, and it was apparent that these concerns were beginning to be heard by her spouse, whom I will call Jim. Jenny's major concern was with Jim's alcohol consumption and resulting irresponsible behavior. Jim admitted to being a binge-drinker and openly stated to Jenny that he would work harder to control himself. She continued to throw attacks, and he continued to acknowledge that his behavior needed to improve. By the end of our session, he was exhausted, and he said, "What more do you want? I said I would change!" I reflected this statement back to Jenny to ensure she had heard what Jim had said. She nodded, and they agreed to give their marriage a few more months to see if it could be salvaged.

The couple returned to see me two months later. Jenny said that she was fed up and wanted out of the relationship. I asked what had been happening. She admitted that Jim had done a great job for six weeks following our last session. "He did more with the kids, did not drink nearly as much, and tried harder to be a family man," she said. In the past couple of weeks, however, he had returned to his old behaviors. Jenny said she was "finished." This time, she brought up a whole host of unexpressed and unresolved hurts and resentments from two to six years earlier. Jim was incensed. He said to Jenny, "I can't please you. I admit that I have gotten off track with the drinking, but I am so tired of hearing about stuff that I did years ago—maybe we should get divorced!" I asked Jenny what her inner dialogue sounded like whenever she was upset. She said it was basically the same *all the time.* She usually returned to thoughts like, "He is so selfish, such a drunk, self-absorbed, and irresponsible." Only once in a while would she think, "Hey, he is participating, so maybe things will work out." Jenny admitted that the inner dialogue was always about the belief that he would *not* be able to make a long-term change. I explained to her that this belief pattern was her defense-coping mechanism.

I worked with Jenny to help her realize that if she continued to believe that Jim was unable to grow, no matter how much he did grow, she would not be able to recognize or validate that. I encouraged her to change the pattern, so that when things were stressful between them, her inner statements could reflect thoughts that soothed and comforted her instead of heightening her upset—thoughts that reflected words and actions based on caring behaviors that Jim had demonstrated in the preceding days. Further, I cautioned Jenny about the belief that Jim would never grow and reminded her of a law of mind that reflects the concept that *as we think (believe), so shall we experience.* Jenny then agreed that in the coming weeks, she would work on creating a new belief and a new soothing statement that she could repeat about both Jim and their marriage.

While it is understandable that we create beliefs, statements, and models of one another based upon past disappointments and fallen expectations, it is equally important for us to examine these defense mechanisms to see their current validity. Many of the destructive thoughts we hold are no longer true, but we fail to review and update these ideas.

The ego loves patterns because it is terrified of the unknown and of change. In the special relationship, the ego, which fluctuates between the past guilt and the future fear, prefers to throw all the unhappiness it can find with our spouse forward to perpetuate this goal. Patterns of behavior become unconscious to our awareness fast, so we need to catch the destructive cycles and disable them through communication and understanding. Here is an example of one of my unconscious patterns: Mornings begin with my morning ritual of waking up and hitting the snooze button, followed by reflection on the dreams I had while sleeping, then a washroom stop and a saunter down the stairs into the kitchen. I then pour my coffee and sit to drink it in my special spot in the loveseat of our reading room. This is largely patterned, unconscious behavior—in short, I do not need to think!

The same is true when we hold fast to inner complaints or destructive assumptions that we do not assess and discuss. Talking makes us aware of what is going on, while inner destructive dialogues that remain unshared hold us captive to past behaviors and criticisms.

All patterns and behaviors are cultivated through repetition, so immediate discussion of any feelings of disappointment and failed expectations is vital to sustain a caring, conscious, and present relationship. For instance, if you are upset because your spouse always leaves his or her clothes on the bedroom floor, it is important to express your feeling to him or her when it happens *the first time*. Your sharing statement would go something like this, "I feel unappreciated and uneasy when I see your clothes all over the bedroom floor because I feel better when our room is tidy." Or you might say, "I work hard, so that we can have a comfortable lifestyle and the clothes that we like, and when I see you leave them on the floor, I feel unappreciated." Notice how both statements are self-reflective: "I feel." They are not driven by "You make me feel." The words *I feel* work as a powerful invitation for communication, which opens your mate to listening, while statements beginning with "You did," "You are," or "You're not" shut your partner down because they feel attacked.

Because we all have histories, there will be past behaviors that will need to be addressed as they resurface. For instance, Allan really dislikes it when I have eaten garlic or Asian spiced foods because of the pungent smell that lingers on my breath. For years, whenever I came home from a dinner and crawled into bed, he would make a disgusted grunt and run for the window and slide it open. Predictably, the topic on the following morning would be about how badly the room smelled, and Allan would make hurtful comments to me. When this "dance" played out again recently, I decided it was time to let Allan know how his words affected me. When he told me again that my breath was awful, I said, "You know, I feel hurt, ashamed, and condemned when you tell me how horrible my breath is." He stood silenced, with a clear look of regret in his eyes. Then he said, "I had no idea that you felt that badly when I said that stuff. Of course, I know that you can't help your breath when you eat those foods—that's why I open the window. I am sorry." I asked, "Do you want me to stop eating them?" He said, "No, of course not." Previously, whenever Allan had commented on my breath, my inner dialogue had been, "He is such a childish jerk," or "What an ---hole!"

With the destructive cycle identified, we can stop it altogether. Allan may forget this in the future, and if he does, I will remind him again of how I feel. I am certain that, after a couple of times, the pattern will end. If, on the other hand, I ignore his next statement of disapproval, I will be just as responsible for the outcome—more hurtful comments. What had become clear was that we both needed to change our words when we were confronted with this issue. We each chose more self-supportive words instead of defensive ones. In the future, mine will be, "It's okay, and we will try again."

Parenting Style Differences

Regardless of whether we are in a blended or traditional nuclear family unit, differences in parenting styles and beliefs are destined to emerge. The dynamics of the parent/child relationship are complex and change with varying levels of awareness and the maturing of both the child and parent. Each party is growing and changing their beliefs based upon experiences, fears, and accomplishments.

What is vital for the parents to agree on are the "house rules," curfews, and disciplinary actions to be implemented when rules are broken. Normally, I suggest to parents to involve children age seven and older in determining the disciplinary actions that should follow the children's misbehavior. My experience is that often one parent will be very strict, while the other will tend to be very soft, so it is the middle ground that is just right! Children seem to know this and, in fact, they tend to choose disciplinary actions more congruent with the middle ground. Children and teenagers do crave behavioral boundaries, since these help them to feel noticed and valued. While reasoning and discussions to explain these boundaries are often effective with younger and prepubescent children, they are not always sufficient for teens, in whose minds the reasoning capacity concerning cause and effect is not yet stabilized, largely due to rapid spurts of brain growth. Agreeing on disciplinary actions before they need to be implemented is sometimes necessary.

As a mother of five, I have found it to be helpful to make the discipline equal to the mistake in terms of its impact. In my home, dishonesty is treated most severely. My teenage boys know to expect harsher consequences for lying or withholding information than for any other mistake they admit to making. This has been their journey with me since birth. Activities like drug and alcohol use on our property come in second!

Allan and I stand united on both these fronts, but we disagree on the amount of chores the kids need to do. In his opinion, I am too soft, whereas I believe that he is too strict, so we try to find middle ground. We are unified, however, on the fact that we want them to do their own laundry, clean their own rooms, clean up after themselves in the kitchen, and do whatever we ask of them.

Where many couples come into struggle is in the way that discipline is implemented. Parents should never be under the influence of anger when they decide upon corrective measures for the inappropriate behavior of their children, but should remain calm and collected. An example might be to say in a poised way: "You were caught with beer in your room, so you will be grounded for a week." This is more effective than an angry statement such as, "I found beer in your room, and you know we don't allow that. You never listen. If you can't live by my rules, you should get out!"

The above example depicts the differing styles in which Allan and I tend to implement disciplinary actions when these are called for. The differences are primarily due to the fact that I am a woman and Allan is a man. I like to use gentle, nurturing-style enforcement, while Allan just wants the kids to get the point. He wants them to respect authority and the hierarchy of command. He feels that this is his roost, and they need to respect the rules of the roost! While I do not agree with Allan's model of discipline, I realize that it does help to teach my boys how to function in the world of business, which is still largely masculine in nature. To be effective in such an environment, it is important to be able to work within a structured system and respect organizational hierarchies. I also recognize that the softer I seem to be, the harder Allan becomes. Therefore, I can strive to find middle ground, so that Allan can do the same.

It is critical that both parents learn to speak clearly about what bothers them and avoid statements that are degrading and disrespectful. For instance, if my sons are watching television and the volume is turned on too loudly, my response to them should be, "Please turn down the volume," rather than "Are you deaf?"

Well-rounded kids need a healthy mix of support and challenge, feminine and masculine, calm and stormy energies. Most of all, kids need to see emotionally healthy, caring parents who respect and trust one another with their children's care and rearing.

Trust—Financial and Emotional

Some of the most powerful emotions that I needed to encounter, reflect on, and transcend were those connected with the areas of money and motherhood. Both were arenas that harbored forgotten memories and feelings of powerlessness and betrayal. Let's explore each of those arenas in hopes that my story can lend insight to your situation.

Allan and I started off doing quite well at the task of blending a family. For several months, Allan was enamored with my two young sons—then ages five and four. He spoke of the importance of winning my heart in part by caring and nurturing for my boys. He was right, and as long as I felt that he was caring for and nurturing them, I could tolerate the discipline he dished out now and then.

Within a few years, however, his resentment towards the kids built up, and in time I stopped trusting him with their emotional safety. His resentment came largely from feeling imprisoned by my unspoken yet energetically communicated threat to leave if he did not perform the way I wanted him to in regards to parenting. I was oblivious to the impact that my unspoken threat had on him. In a way, I was saying to Allan, "You can provide finances, nurture, attention, and be a role model, but you cannot learn how to parent, because that is *my* job." In short, I was thinking I had all the insights and wisdom, and Allan had none. After all, he had not had any biological children, so he could not possibly understand them as I did.

As a 40-year-old bachelor at the time when Allan and I got together, he was ill-informed about the gut-wrenching, self-exposing, and emotionally taxing experience of stepfatherhood that lay ahead for him. Equally naïve at that time, I needed to do some deep soul-searching and own my crippling demand for power over Allan in the carefully disguised role of mother. It was as if I were saying to him, "Hey, buddy, when it comes to money, you may have control, but when it comes to raising the kids, I'll hold the hammer!" This approach was creating emotional paralysis. We needed a better way.

The better way began with my openly confessing that I did not trust Allan with the emotional well-being of my kids. In fact, I unearthed an unrecognized belief that *no man* was trustworthy of caring for and nurturing either a woman's or her children's feelings. What a belief that was to own! In my heart, I knew this was not true, and so I needed to heal that belief, and Allan was right by my side to help me do so.

The next step for me to take was to decide if I could attempt to trust Allan for a while, to see what happened. I concluded that what I had been doing previously had not worked, so reason pointed to giving him a chance. I did, and he managed beautifully. Although there were moments when I was terrified of the word exchanges between my sons and him, they all seemed to be figuring things out quite nicely without my meddling and controlling their behaviors. Once I had faced my greatest fear, which was to lose my kids because of Allan's behavior, I was free. I decided that if I could not trust Allan with the emotional and behavioral needs of the boys, I should leave the relationship. If the boys moved out because they were mad at Allan, then so be it. My old way was not working—neither Allan nor the boys had respect for one another. Neither had a voice to say what they were really feeling; neither side was happy. So I knew in my heart that if I were to keep binding Allan's behaviors, words, and disciplinary actions with the boys, our family would never develop the intimacy I ached to have. I surrendered to Allan and prayed for strength and wisdom, but most of all, I prayed for the courage to keep my mouth shut.

Allan told me that once I uncuffed him through trusting him a little, he could communicate differently with the children. He reminded me that, after all, I had learned to parent through experience. I had made mistakes and everyone survived, so why not give him the same chance? I did, and am still doing so each day. Trust is growing, and we are all doing better than before.

If I was paralyzed by fear in the arena of family and emotions, then the counterbalance to my fear was Allan's fear of being taken by me financially. This journey was explored in the chapter on intimacy, so I will not repeat the story here. However, I do want to look at what drives our fear around having our money taken away from us.

In dealing with couples, I see a pattern. The man often controls the money to ensure his seat of power. The woman's power often comes from her sexuality and from being the mother and homemaker. He wants security and freedom. She wants intimacy. He is designed and conditioned to protect and provide financially, and when he does this, he feels power. Because she is starved emotionally, she wants to buy things to feed her hunger. The more she spends, the more frightened he becomes. If finances are not available to do this, and if her work is aligned with her soul's passion, she will gravitate toward overwork to compensate.

Can he keep up? Intuitively, he knows he is not feeding her emotional hunger, but he also does not know how to do it. Unconsciously, he is feeling incompetent, so he works harder to cover these feelings, and to make her happy financially. She spends his hard-earned money, and for a day or so, her ache diminishes. But then, like the sunrise, the hunger returns. In time, she needs more to get rid of the pain, while he begins to resent her never being satisfied. This is a familiar pattern for many.

The next debilitating belief around financial trust between the sexes is the socialized belief that in divorce, the woman always takes the man financially. I find this interesting because statistics actually prove the opposite. The question is, what does a belief like this do in the psyche of a man in an intimate relationship? It cripples it. Allan, who also once believed that one day I would take him "to the cleaners," needed to decide if he treasured our love or the money. He realized that if he could not trust me financially, we could not build a relationship honoring equality. Then, he decided that the money (should I take it) would have been the investment he made to have had a soulful relationship, and he concluded that a soulful relationship was worth the cost.

For many men, their self-identity is in part connected with their money. Their self-worth is woven into their net worth. Women do the same with their children. They often believe that if you reject their child, you are rejecting them. Men feel this way with their earnings. If you do not appreciate and care for the money they bring into the household, you do not appreciate them. A man who feels that his wife spends his income carelessly is a man with a Vise-Grip on his wallet!

Couples need to discuss their money, the trust issues surrounding their money, and the deep feelings of greed and possessiveness that are fostered when the money is in jeopardy of being minimized or taken away. We are all conditioned to believe that money is power, and so the person with the most money holds the hammer. While this may be true, rest assured that the money-constrained partner also has a "hammer."

While money is one expression of power, it is not the only one. And in every household, there is an equality of power at all times; it is just not always recognized as such. While many therapists and negotiators believe in power imbalances between the parties, I do not, and identifying the many expressions or tools of power you have is crucial to the success of the soulful union. Here are some other "power tools" to explore: sex, being a primary caregiver, inheritance money, homemaking, holding title to the home or business, holding social power, having media influence, bookkeeping, using anger or rage, threatening, playing the victim, playing the helpless child, holding on to a mistake, and the use of guilt.

Trust is immeasurable in its value. It is a cornerstone of the sacred union we all deserve, so if there are any arenas where trust was broken, work hard to discuss them. Then begin rebuilding the trust by placing malleable boundaries around the issue. Make an agreement to not spend large amounts of money without checking in with your partner. Prioritize where surplus cash is going to be directed or spent. Make promises to each other to be respectful of money and be gentle with each other's concerns around it. Agree to take little steps until bigger ones feel safe, and be honest to ask for the boundaries you feel are necessary to begin letting go of the money.

For instance, if the idea of equally dividing and sharing the surplus cash or savings seems frightening at first, start by sharing one quarter or one eighth of it. As trust builds through seeing that your partner does not run off and blow the money, share more, until equality in finances is achieved. Lastly, if there is one partner making considerably more money than the other, create a budget that must be adhered to by both. Then put all the income from both people in one pot, and pay all the household bills and personal expenses from that pot. Next, divide equally the difference and put it either into a joint account, or put each half into two separate savings accounts to which both spouses have access. Lastly, pay all large-ticket items or events, such as vacations, out of those accounts equally.

This exercise in money management may seem outdated, but it works for two primary reasons. First, it balances financial power; and second, it keeps us conscious and accountable to our spouse for our spending patterns. Transparency in financial matters builds trust.

In my two previous marriages, there were few, if any, fights about money. Part of the reason was probably that we didn't have much of it to compete for. The other reason we did not argue was because we were transparent with what was earned and spent, and the larger expenditures were agreed upon. In those relationships, there was just enough income to live paycheck to paycheck, and we shared a joint bank account.

This all changed when I married Allan. He was not interested in sharing a single account, and neither was I. I decided that I was not about to lose my credit rating or financial history to Allan. Experience had shown me that many women had no credit history after the divorce. After my own divorces, I shared the experience of many of my friends who discovered that, although they had managed the household income and paid the bills on time, they were not viewed as financially responsible. I didn't want to go through that same experience again, and therefore Allan and I decided to live autonomous financial lives. This worked for about seven years, but in time I grew angry, because he controlled our finances.

When I invited Allan to explore the idea of changing this, he became defensive. At the root of his fear was the assumption that I was going to spend all *his* money. Now, don't get me wrong. Allan is a very generous man, but he needed to have the power to hand out the amount he felt safe to share—this was his boundary. However, I would not settle unless he could agree to share our wealth equally. It took about three years to arrive at this point. We moved from his writing me "bonus" checks, to a joint account, to equal sharing of everything.

With the decision to share everything equally came the absolute necessity to be transparent in all spending. Each had to share with the other what was spent on personal items—our "toys"—and for me the most difficult disclosure was what I spent on the kids and my grandson. This was unnerving for me, as my ego screamed, "This is crazy; you make a very nice income and are entitled to spend as you see fit. You work hard and are responsible with your finances—why do you need to get his permission?" My reply was, "Because we are partners!"

In the beginning, Allan was uncomfortable with my way of keeping a record of the funds I earned and spent. He balanced his checkbook to the penny and found my more liberal approach of rounding off balances to within a hundred dollars or so to be irresponsible and frightening. He didn't want to be connected with it. I appreciated his fears, yet did not buy into them for myself. Unforeseen circumstances do happen in my life, and when they arise, I need to manifest the funds required to take care of them, and

I always do. I affirm my abundance, and then I trust. The result is usually an increase in appointments, accelerated book sales, or an oversold workshop that I am about to teach. The point here is that the money always comes when I stay in a spirit of certainty and appreciation, rather than fear and lack.

Allan has a Scottish mother who values every cent. Beneath her frugality is the fear of not having enough money to remain independent. Like Allan, she is afraid of coming up short should something unforeseen happen. She and Allan both need to have a financial "buffer" to ensure they can handle a setback, should one occur. Allan and his mom, like all of us, like to feel safe, free, and independent, and particularly free from needing anyone else financially!

I have always been trusting and generous with money. I see it as an energy to exchange for goods and services, and, really, I rarely feel that it is missing. I also have surplus cash in my account to cover any unexpected expenses or setbacks, but not because I am afraid. I do it so I need not micromanage my cash flow. I simply believe that money always comes, and so it does. I have great respect for money, and I work hard to attract and share it, but I am not imprisoned by it. Allan, after many years of being afraid of not having enough, is beginning to learn the same—to keep a surplus, but not worry so much about tracking every cent.

When it comes to balancing the household checkbook, that is Allan's department. He is better at it than I am, and he enjoys doing it. He keeps an impeccable ledger listing each check and every payment made, so that we can budget each year. I do not touch or interfere with this important work; I appreciate it.

Here is how we handle our finances: Allan takes a portion of our combined income and puts it into a household checking account, out of which all household expenditures are paid. Then Allan and I each have a joint savings account with half of the total surplus savings in each account. Before these savings are deposited, we set aside monies to be given to charities, pay down mortgages, and invest a portion in low-risk ventures and another in RRSPs.

So, if we wanted to buy a new piece of furniture, renovate the house, or upgrade either of our wardrobes, we would discuss the purchase, agree to it, and then share the cost equally from each of our savings accounts. If either of us receives unexpected income, we divide it equally and deposit the amounts into each of our savings accounts. Every year, we sit down and draft a budget and plan the income and expenditures for the following year. Expenditures would include items like education, training, property taxes, yard maintenance, and so on. Then, like clockwork, every year, unexpected expenditures arise, and we adapt and reprioritize the monies budgeted. As a result of this process, we both grow in our maturity, generosity, and willingness to be transparent in our spending.

In many ways, a romantic union is like a business partnership. Each needs to agree to take ownership of, and responsibility for, certain duties. However, both partners need to have the skills and abilities to do the others person's job, such as vacuuming or taking out the trash. This is necessary to sustain equality, minimize fear, and be aware of the financial situation should one of you become incapacitated or pass away. For instance, I used to be the only one who shopped for groceries. I knew where to shop in order to save, how to bulk-buy, and the exact cost of everything, while Allan did not. Now, due to shifting career obligations, Allan does most of our grocery shopping. As a result, we are both skilled in this area and can plan and budget without arguing about the cost of groceries.

When it comes to learning about finance, investing, and money management, many of us cringe, but in doing so, we can learn to appreciate the up- and downsides connected with these matters. Further, we gain wisdom and feel more competent and self-assured in investing energies towards learning. Fear comes with the unknown, and mastery with experience, so start asking and participating!

Assuming and Withholding

While we have already addressed the topic of keeping secrets and learning to share them, we have not yet addressed the issue of making untrue assumptions and thus withholding information. The ego is not interested in our being vulnerable or transparent. In fact, in the precious moments we have the courage to be either, the ego ceases to exist. In any moment that the ego is dispelled, we are sharing our oneness with our mate, and our unity is another experience in which the ego has no interest. Both vulnerability and openness are, in the ego's view, extreme positions of weakness, so it warns us not to go there. However, if we want a sacred, soulful union, we must. In this section, we will search for our ego-fostered assumptions and the natural withholding that occurs from them. Let me share a story.

For two years, a client of mine, Jess, shared with me that she believed her marriage was coming to an end. Not because there was anything really wrong with it—she felt it was just completing because she and her husband had grown in all the ways they could. "Our contract is ending," she said. Jess was not particularly upset with these feelings of closure; she just wanted to explore what all the reasons for them might be. I agreed to work with her on this.

Our two-year exploration began by my asking some questions to identify where Jess and Jack shared values, priorities, and goals and where they didn't. We determined that Jess was deeply focused on her career, primarily because it made her feel financially independent from Jack. This was a revelation for her. Next, we discussed her deep desire to pursue spirituality and what it was in particular that she got in return. In time, we discovered that she achieved emotional maturing through her self-exploration and beliefs. She also made close friendships and gained a sense of personal power. What was of real insight, however, was that through the quest of developing her spirituality, she often participated in caring, intimate conversations with her male friends. Intimacy was something that Jess had been craving from Jack for the past 14 years. It became clear to Jess that she had unconsciously found the intimacy she wanted through these conversations with her male friends, so her need to create it with Jack was dissipating over time. Next, we determined that she was terrified of standing on her own financially, and since they had recently come into some substantial money, the reasons for her desire to end the marriage were becoming clearer.

I asked Jess to invite Jack to attend a session with her, so that we could see how he was feeling about the marriage. Jess was hesitant. She assured me that Jack would not attend such a meeting and that, in fact, this was in part why she felt that their "dance" was done. I reminded her that if she could connect his participation to something of value to him, he would come.

Jess decided that, since Jack had been complaining about their lack of sex, she could dangle promises for more sex if he came. Jack agreed to come, but he was definitely apprehensive. He thought Jess' interest in personal and spiritual growth was somewhat strange, and he wanted me to know that he was not looking to be converted. I agreed to honor his concern.

During our meeting, I began asking Jack some questions; I wanted to see if Jess was accurate in some of the assumptions she was making. I asked Jack if he wanted more emotional closeness with Jess. He said that he did, but did not know how to achieve this. He confessed that he had tried several things, such as taking her out and buying her gifts to create some closeness, but that this was effective for only about a week...then they were back to where they had started.

I asked Jack if he held any beliefs about God. He said he believed in God, but that he did not want to have religion shoved down his throat, as had occurred when he was young and being raised in the Lutheran Church. I asked him if he knew the difference between practicing spirituality and a religion. He said he viewed them as the same. I wanted to know if Jack had ever asked Jess about her beliefs, and he said he had done so once, but that Jess was vague about what she believed, and so he assumed the subject was off limits for her.

I asked Jack whether, if he knew that sexual intimacy would improve as a result of his taking interest in Jess's spiritual pursuits and her career, he would be willing to participate in conversations about them, to which he agreed. Lastly, I asked Jack if he was aware of the fact that Jess had been contemplating the ending of their marriage, and if he was happy in his marriage. His reply was no to both questions, but he said that he still loved Jess.

Jess was stunned as she took in Jack's words. She said that it had never actually occurred to her to share her feelings of wanting out of the marriage, her desire for wanting more intimacy, or her need to share her personal growth and spiritual realizations with Jack. She said she had assumed that he would not care.

This story magnifies for us that what we hide will eventually run our lives. All our inner hidden beliefs and assumptions need to be reviewed and shared if we hope to mature the marriage. In my work with couples like Jess and Jack, I have found that the stuff we are withholding is the same stuff that will set us free.

This also applies when we withhold from our spouse the information that we have been unfaithful. My experience has shown that seven out of ten marriages endure the experience of infidelity, while only four out of ten people are willing to admit to the incident.

If you have been sexually unfaithful to your spouse, the burning question in your heart may well be, "Do I continue to withhold this information?" The answer is dependent upon two things: If in years past, you were unfaithful to your mate, but have since repaired the causes of your unfaithfulness, I do not recommend you tell your spouse about it in order to appease your guilt. Your feelings of guilt over being sexually unfaithful are not necessarily going to ease because you shared the information, but your understanding of, and compassion for, whatever it was that triggered the behavior, and then changing that behavior, will. The desire you feel beneath the guilt is the spirit's yearning for honesty, both with yourself and your partner. The truth is that your innocence is as unassailable as that of your spouse, regardless of anything that happened. If your actions were based on ego, fear, and lack, they are indicative of perceived unfulfilled needs you were feeling that were not openly shared with your partner, which led you to look outside the relationship for fulfillment. If in the past you have not been willing to be fully honest and share your needs and desires with your spouse, use the memory of the infidelity to catalyze the desire to do so now. Share with your spouse your desire for full openness and honesty as an act towards creating deeper levels of intimacy, which is undoubtedly what your real self craves.

If, however, you are asked directly if you have been unfaithful, I suggest that you admit the transgression and share the reasons why you think the infidelity occurred. Remember our addiction to, and overprotectiveness of, the body, as well as possessiveness, are a reaction from the ego, rather than the spirit. If your spouse feels unable to use the information to strengthen and deepen the relationship, you must trust that, from the soul's perspective, the purpose of the relationship has been accomplished.

My experience shows that most relationships can endure the many differing forms of infidelity that touch it. In fact, infidelity can become a powerful transformational tool towards creating a soulful, rather than special, relationship. This is accomplished if the exploration of this act is done through the lens of presumed mutual innocence on the part of all parties involved. What is crucial to the success of turning infidelity into trust is to see the act as a symptom, rather than a cause, of a much deeper issue. Honesty and transparency on the part of the couple are the salve that heals this turbulent experience.

The many differing forms of infidelity include engaging in sexual fantasies about a particular person, e.g., a co-worker or neighbor, certain types of Internet chatting, and kissing and petting with friends or co-workers at social parties while inebriated. When these actions and events emerge, they do bring with them the gift of testing the emotional integrity of our union. And although we may at times fail the test, we can use the failure to recommit with even more vigilance to the sacredness of the matrimonial bond in the future.

Prioritizing and "Self-Fullness"

In our soulful relationship, it is imperative that we stay current with the priorities that come out of our voids—the things we feel are missing. Things like feeling important, valued, and heard. Things like time for the relationship, a vacation, or time alone with the kids. Or maybe it is assets like a new home, a new carpet, car, or wardrobe.

When we admit these needs, we may feel that we are selfish. However, if we do not voice and express our yearnings, we will be perceived as selfish instead of self-full. To be self-full means that we value and fulfill our needs first, so that we can give from that fullness into the world. We prioritize our basic needs to be met, and respect our mate's needs to be met as well. When basic needs go unmet for too long, we become cranky, mean, emotionally distanced, and unavailable to joyfully meet the needs of others.

When we do not honor our needs as much as the needs of those around us, we will begin to feel used and underappreciated. We feel this way because we have devalued our needs with respect to our spouse and our children. The result of such activity over time is crippling to the emotional and sexual intimacy of the union, so if this is what you have been doing, please consider changing it now. This change can be assisted greatly by replacing the idea that caring for oneself is selfish, and instead seeing it as being supportive of self-fullness. When we feel plentiful, we are able to give from our feelings of abundance.

As a natural result of the evolution of two souls, which in turn matures a marital union, we will be undergoing constant change as we unearth our fears to one another and to ourselves. As we grow in self-love, we naturally want more on all levels of experience. This "more" includes financial freedom, emotional connections, time, and space, until one magical day we outgrow those desires because we discover that all we need is in us. Eventually, we awaken to the remembrance that we are an abundant, unlimited, radiant, eternal, and all-inclusive self.

When we welcome the oceans of feelings that always arise with the discoveries of the once disabling and disempowering beliefs that we had adopted, the ego is divorced. And although a person may at times feel very selfish in stating their needs and requesting them to be both heard and met, it is nevertheless important to do so.

I have witnessed countless marriages die due to the fear that expressing one party's needs will send their partner running. The truth is that the soulful union is strengthened with transparency and honesty, but it is most surely weakened by secrecy and withholding. And since the ego does not want you to experience love, it will scream at you that you should not ask for what you need, share your fears, or admit your feelings of powerlessness. The ego will encourage you to keep silent in order to save the relationship, but this will not save the union—it will make it go numb. The truth is that admitting to our mate that we do have feelings of powerlessness and fear is an effective recipe for transforming the special relationship into a soulful one.

Chapter Eleven

The Soulmates' Final Dance

One of the questions I am most frequently asked in my work with couples or individuals looking for a deeply intimate relationship is, "How will I know my soulmate?" The question brings with it a powerful belief, held by many people, that there is one special being who is our true soulmate. While it is true that when our soul was created, there was another soul that was born with us—our "birth-soulmate"—it is not true that we can have a soulful love union only with this birth-soulmate.

The birth-soulmate is a being that has the same light and sound vibration as we have. When we encounter this being, powerfully vulnerable feelings arise, and the ego persona vanishes. We literally melt into one being. The divine love that arises from the melting into one surpasses human understanding. The feelings and the experience transcend humanness and catapult the soul pair into the memory of their authentic selves as spirit, rather than bodies. When we are with our "birth-soulmate," a state of being that is totally accepting and appreciative of the other is present. There is no longer a necessity to awaken to one's true self because encountering our birth-soulmate will jolt us into that awareness. Our awakening up until then will have been a gradual process and will have occurred through our interaction with many different souls, so that we could be prepared for the final dance with our birth-soulmate.

When we have learned to love and appreciate all traits and characteristics of our closest relationships, particularly those of our spouse, we are finally ready to dance with our birth-soulmate. Through our appreciation of all sides of others, we will have appreciated and integrated all of our own shadow sides. Between the birth-soulmates, there is no need for healing unloved parts, no ego, and no competition. In the union of birth-soulmates, the partners are quite literally powerless, defenseless, and transparent with each other.

The union with the birth-soulmate is indicative of our nearing the stage where we will no longer require the earthly experience. We will have transitioned beyond any desire for the special relationship union or its ego-based dynamics. Remember the purpose of the world is to offer us a substitute for love, and the special relationship is the form that the substitute comes in. So, when we have learned, through each relationship, to choose soulful rather than special relationship premises, we will have prepared one another for the encounter with our birth-soulmate.

Because we are both preparing and being prepared for the last dance—the one with our birth-soulmate—the people with whom we are preparing are sacred and should be honored as such. We could not possibly be ready for the complete melting of all of our defenses, which naturally occurs when we meet our birth-soulmate, without our "preparatory" sacred encounters with those who are in our life now.

Two Souls—One Light

The following text is excerpted from my book Our Cosmic Dance *(The Art of Blending Families and Difficult Relationships; the Phoenix Coaching and Transformation Corporation, 2004).*

During my accelerated period of awakening that occurred during a time when Allan and I were briefly separated, it seemed that I had an open door to the *Akashic Records*, also known as *The Book of Life*. I asked some of life's deepest questions then, and it was made clear to me that the Great Orchestrating Design does not wish to keep anything from Its Creations. And, as Dr John Demartini states so well in his book *The Breakthrough Experience*™: *A Revolutionary New Approach to Personal Transformation*, "The quality of the answers we receive is based upon the quality of the questions we ask!"

At one point during this period, I pondered in my heart the question of how souls were made, and to my amazement, I was shown the answer. Since words are often inadequate to properly describe the wonders of the Great Orchestrating Design, the process of how souls are created was shown to me in telepathically communicated imagery. I shut my eyes and saw what appeared to be a galaxy, although it was not really that—a galaxy is just the closest thing I have to compare to what I saw. There was a velvety blackness, and out of it came incredible bursts of light, which then split. I understood the light to be a "beingness," and it was somehow androgynous. Then, quite magically, it refracted out of itself a twin light that I perceived to be male or female, depending upon which dominant traits or qualities it sustained in its presence or being. I sensed that these two mirror reflections were in communication, although I heard nothing audible. I sensed that each was also a mirror reflection and expression of something greater. Not in the sense of this being something better, but rather something more ordered, conscious, and intelligent.

The soul looked somewhat like a star—but not quite. There was a feeling of a chorus of attending "light-being figures" witnessing the process. It seemed not really as much of a physical phenomenon as a mystical one.

I sensed that this pair of souls was to embark upon an infinite journey, and would one day be one of these attending beings. I felt the attending beings were like parents or midwives—this seems to be the closest possible explanation. I knew somehow that each of these souls was to separate from its partner and dance an infinite series of dances until there would be no part of themselves, or what appeared as others, that they did not love, understand, and appreciate. Time to accomplish this task had no meaning, for the certainty of the accomplishment was inherent.

I sensed that these two beings were alike, yet opposite. They were drawn to, and expressing in opposition to, each other. I knew that both were whole in and of themselves, but since they were of "One Light," they would one day return to each other fully loving, appreciating, and understanding all things of the flesh. When this would be accomplished, they would then reunite and together be able to create "Light" that reflected their soul.

Each would journey to the land of flesh and live under its illusory spells of separation and loss. Each would encounter other souls who were contracted to help each of them fully love and appreciate all aspects of themselves—both the feminine and the masculine. Since there were indeed things these "young souls" did not yet understand and appreciate about themselves and the Great Orchestrating Design, there was much to learn, and many souls to dance with. However, because energy is never really created or destroyed, but rather transformed into higher and higher states of awareness and order, each soul would always be surrounded by the components of its mate. When the soul recognized its mate in the many and no longer yearned for what it already had, a sound "like the sound of a trumpet" would sound in heaven, and each soul would begin the journey back towards each other.

Because there were such differences in what each would learn to love about itself and in the rate at which this was to be accomplished, the possibility of encountering yet not recognizing each "self" was apparent. Therefore, there were three deities ordered to attend to each soul pair. The deities were those of *Necessity, Compassion*, and *Choice*. Their purpose was to assist the pair to encounter and embrace their most fractured and disowned parts, just as they had once helped me to learn how to love and to forgive the belief in my guilt. To the degree that each individual soul could integrate itself, to that same degree did it also facilitate that same integration for its mate, even though this mate was dancing a different dance at that particular time. In other words, any advancement by either soul would have an immediate effect on its mate.

The soul pair would rarely be together in the flesh, although they would be able to help each other from the nonphysical dimension. The final return to each other was sped up only through the increased awareness that there was no part or characteristic unworthy of loving and appreciating within them.

The vision and dialogue ended, and I stopped looking for my mate, by whom I knew myself to be always inseparably surrounded.

Epilogue

Soul to Soul

Who is the mate that is the mirror of my being with whom I am destined to dance?

It is the one who is empowered to reveal both my deepest love and my darkest fear.

I am the soul that is called upon to dance in this life with you—I am your soulmate.

Through this sacred union, we will reveal our true beings as we slowly carve away at our illusory selves. At times, this will feel painful, scary, and unnerving, and yet at other times, it will feel courageous, purposeful, and just.

Why do you stay when my words can, at times, sting like poison on an open wound?

Why is it that you see a radiance in me which I cannot yet recognize?

I stay because I am hopelessly in love with your real self; therefore, your power-hungry, fear-driven words cannot obscure my vision or my love.

How does your unshakable love for me create a womb in which I can find my innocence?

How is it that you have become strong enough to so often let me be right?

My love is a womb which births unity, transparency, vulnerability, intimacy, and truth, and therefore it births you. You are right because you are love.

From where do you receive your reward for the task of being my mate?

What gives you the strength to delve deeply within your being, and then offer that self to me?

In my giving is also my receiving; after all, having and being are two equal sides of the same self. To give to you is to give to and awaken Myself.

What was the purpose of our dance?

The purpose was to heal our belief in lack, limitation, guilt, fear, punishment, autonomy, and specialness, but most important of all, it was to heal the belief that we could ever be separated from love and thus each other.

What will happen when the music stops and our dance is done?

When our dance is done, a new partner will arrive. The music to which you dance will then be that of your eternally joined souls. Then Heaven will sing along in your song of Gratitude to me.

The Last Dance

Our final Dance is one in which we learn that the dance, the dance floor, the music, and the participants are all ultimately we ourselves. They are all projections of our deeply-seated guilt, born of the belief that we could dance apart from God. Miraculously, however, through the dances we *remember*, and thus the dream dance slips silently into the nothingness from which it came. You see, in the Last Dance, we return to love, being formless, timeless, and spaceless; we remember who we are, and that our identity is unalterable. We awaken, having learned that the deepest meaning of love is to acknowledge that we are all wholly innocent, brilliant beings freed from the belief that we ever separated from our Source, our Substance, and our Supply.

To keep your marriage brimming,
With love in the loving cup,
Whenever you're wrong admit it,
Whenever you're right shut up.

Ogden Nash,
To Keep Your Marriage Brimming

About the Author

Moreah Ragusa, RFM, is a psychotherapist, registered family mediator, marriage counselor, corporate coach, and a popular speaker and seminar leader. She has been a student and teacher of the internationally acclaimed spiritual text *A Course in Miracles* for more than fifteen years and is recognized for her ability to illuminate and clarify its teachings.

Deeply committed to helping others on their life path, Moreah is the founder and president of the Phoenix Coaching and Transformation Corporation in Calgary, Alberta. The company offers life mastery strategies to reveal each individual's inherent wisdom, prosperity, freedom, and power.

As the author and teacher of the Emotional Transitions Process™, Ms. Ragusa is also vice president in charge of Emotional Transitions for Fairway Divorce Solutions Ltd.

Moreah is the author of two previous books on spiritual transformation. The first, *Rediscovering Your Authentic Self,* based on *A Course in Miracles,* has helped many to understand the connection of thought and experience. The second, *Our Cosmic Dance*, is a candid autobiography offered as a teaching model for personal and relationship growth.

Passionate about sharing her deep understanding of spiritual truths and the human journey, Moreah has appeared on numerous radio and television shows.

Moreah is currently working on her next book, *The New Divorce Paradigm*, slated for publication in Summer 2006.

Other Books by Moreah Ragusa

- **Rediscovering Your Authentic Self**
  Achieving self-empowerment through spiritual mastery (based on *A Course in Miracles*)
  Also available on CD in audio book format; abridged.

- **Our Cosmic Dance**
  Autobiography and teaching model for personal and relationship growth

CDs by Moreah Ragusa

- **Relationships: Our Journey to Enlightenment**
  Recording of a live lecture series on relationships

- **Understanding A Course in Miracles**
  Recording of a live lecture series, discussing the meaning of various topics explored in *A Course in Miracles*, including love, forgiveness, guilt, and atonement

- **Creating Mastery in Your Life**
  Recording of a live lecture series, discussing topics such as how to apply the laws of love to different areas of your life, including the areas of money, relationships, and health

Contact Information

To order Moreah's books and CDs, for information on our services, or to book Moreah for a lecture, conference, seminar, or retreat, please visit our
Web site: www.thephoenixcoaching.com
           info@thephoenixcoaching.com
Or call: 403-278-3700

Looking back,
may I be filled with gratitude;

Looking forward,
may I be filled with hope;

Looking upward,
may I be aware of strength;

Looking inward,
may I find peace.

Author unknown